Study Guide

Chapters 1-9

College Accounting

Twenty-second Edition

James A. Heintz, DBA, CPA
Professor of Accounting
School of Business
University of Kansas

Robert W. Parry, Jr., Ph.D.
Professor of Accounting
Kelley School of Business
Indiana University

CENGAGE Learning®

Australia • Brazil • Mexico • Singapore • United Kingdom • United States

For product information and technology assistance, contact us at **Cengage Learning Academic Resource Center, 1-800-423-0563**.

For permission to use material from this text or product, submit all requests online at **www.cengage.com/permissions**. Further permissions questions can be emailed to **permissionrequest@cengage.com**.

ISBN: 978-1-305-66767-9

Cengage Learning
20 Channel Center Street
Boston, MA 02210
USA

Cengage Learning is a leading provider of customized learning solutions with employees residing in nearly 40 different countries and sales in more than 125 countries around the world. Find your local representative at **www.cengage.com**.

Cengage Learning products are represented in Canada by Nelson Education, Ltd.

To learn more about Cengage Learning Solutions, visit **www.cengage.com**.

Purchase any of our products at your local college store or at our preferred online store **www.cengagebrain.com**.

Printed in the United States of America
Print Number: 01   Print Year: 2015

Table of Contents

CHAPTER 1
INTRODUCTION TO ACCOUNTING

LEARNING OBJECTIVES

Chapter 1 is designed to introduce you to accounting—its purpose, process, and career opportunities. Businesses that keep good accounting records benefit in many ways. Users of accounting information are able to make sound decisions, which will affect the business's future. Accounting offers many career opportunities, some of which are entry level and task oriented and others that involve decision making and planning.

Objective 1.   Describe the purpose of accounting.
   Accounting is the process by which businesses keep track of daily transactions and determine how the business is doing. Accounting provides needed information for its many users, from owners to government agencies and others.

Objective 2.   Describe the accounting process.
   The accounting process contains six major steps.
   Step 1   Analyzing: Looking at information available and figuring out what to do with it. This first step in the accounting process usually occurs when the business receives some type of information, such as a bill, that needs to be properly entered into the business's records. This first step also involves deciding if the piece of information should result in an accounting entry or not.
   Step 2   Recording: Entering the information, manually or via a computer, into the accounting system.
   Step 3   Classifying: Grouping like items together.
   Step 4   Summarizing: Aggregating many similar events to provide information that is easy to understand.
   Step 5   Reporting: Communicating the results, such as profit or loss, commonly using tables of numbers to tell the financial status of the business.
   Step 6   Interpreting: Examining the financial statements to evaluate the financial health of the business.

Objective 3.   Define GAAP and describe the process used by FASB to develop these principles.
   Generally accepted accounting principles (GAAP) are the rules that businesses must follow when preparing financial statements. The Securities and Exchange Commission (SEC) has the legal power to make these rules for firms listed on one of the U.S. stock exchanges. However, the SEC has delegated this responsibility to the Financial Accounting Standards Board (FASB).

FASB takes the following steps to develop an accounting standard:
   1. The issue is placed on FASB's agenda.
   2. After researching an issue, FASB issues a Preliminary Views document to offer the pros and cons of the accounting alternatives and to invite others to comment.
   3. To gather additional views on the issue, the Board often holds public hearings around the country.
   4. Following these hearings, the Board issues an exposure draft. This document explains the rules that FASB believes firms should follow in accounting for this event.
   5. After considering feedback on the exposure draft, the Board issues an Accounting Standards Update which amends the FASB Accounting Standards Codification.

Objective 4.   Define three types of business ownership structures.
   Businesses can be classified according to who owns them and the specific way they are organized. A sole proprietorship is owned by one person who assumes all risks for the business and makes all business decisions. A partnership is owned by two or more persons who share the risks and decision making. Corporations have many owners (shareholders) whose risk is limited to their investment and who have little influence in business decisions.

Objective 5.   Classify different types of businesses by activities.

Businesses also can be classified by the type of service or product they provide. A service business provides a service, a merchandising business purchases a product from another business to sell, and a manufacturing business makes a product to sell.

Objective 6.   Identify career opportunities in accounting.

Accounting has varied and diverse opportunities, depending on the education and experience of the worker, the type of business, and the accounting processes used within the business.

Accounting clerks record, sort, and file accounting information. Bookkeepers supervise clerks, help with daily accounting work, and summarize information. Para-accountants provide many accounting, auditing, or tax services under the direct supervision of an accountant.

Public accountants offer services such as auditing, tax advice, management advisory services, and forensic accounting services. Under the Sarbanes-Oxley Act, however, they may not provide audit and management advisory services to the same company. Further, audit and tax services may be provided to the same company only if preapproved by the audit committee of the company.

Managerial accountants offer services to private businesses, such as designing accounting information systems, general accounting, cost accounting, budgeting, tax accounting, and internal auditing. Government and not-for-profit organizations also employ accountants.

Accounting is a professional field, which includes organizations and certifications for those who pass examinations and have relevant work experience.

REVIEW QUESTIONS

Instructions: Analyze each of the following items carefully before writing your answer in the column at the right.

Question	**Answer**

LO 1   1. The purpose of accounting is to provide current information to users. For each user below, briefly describe what type of information is needed.

     a.   Owners (present and future)

     b.   Managers who make decisions for the business

     c.   Creditors (present and future)

     d.   Government agencies (state, local, and national)

LO 5   2. A travel agency is an example of this type of business. .... _____

LO 4   3. The ownership structure where owners share risks and decision making is called a(n) _____. .... _____

LO 5   4. A(n) _____ business makes a product to sell. .... _____

LO 5   5. A business that purchases a product from another business to sell to customers is called a(n) _____ business. .... _____

LO 4   6. Under the _____ ownership structure, the owner's personal assets can be taken to pay creditors. .... _____

LO 3   7. The Financial Accounting Standards Board develops procedures and guidelines called _____ to be followed in the accounting process. _____

LO 3 **8.** The following actions are taken by FASB when developing an accounting standard. Indicate the proper sequence of events by placing a 1 through 5 in the space provided.

Step

_____ The Accounting Standards Update is issued which amends the FASB Accounting Standards Codification.

_____ Public hearings are held.

_____ An exposure draft is issued.

_____ The issue is placed on FASB's agenda.

_____ A Preliminary Views document is issued.

LO 4 **9.** The owners' risk is usually limited to their initial investment in this type of ownership structure. .... _____

LO 6 **10.** Is a public accounting firm permitted to provide audit and tax services to a publicly held company?... _____

LO 6 **11.** By meeting education and experience requirements and passing an examination, a public accountant can achieve recognition as a(n) _____ . _____

LO 6 **12.** The segment of accounting practice that includes fraud detection, fraud prevention, litigation support, business valuation, expert witness services, and other investigative activities is known as _____ . ... _____

LO 2 **13.** The six major steps of the accounting process are listed in the box at the right. In front of each term, write the letter that identifies the correct description provided in the column on the left.

a. The process of entering financial information about events affecting the business

b. Aggregating similar events to provide information that is easy to understand

c. The process of sorting or grouping like things together, rather than merely keeping a simple, diary-like narrative record of numerous and varied transactions

d. The process of determining the effect of various events on the business

e. The process of deciding the importance of the information in various reports

f. The process of communicating the results of operation

_____ Analyzing

_____ Recording

_____ Classifying

_____ Summarizing

_____ Reporting

_____ Interpreting

CHAPTER 2
ANALYZING TRANSACTIONS:
THE ACCOUNTING EQUATION

LEARNING OBJECTIVES

Chapter 2 continues the introductory discussion of accounting—its elements, equation, and transactions. The accounting equation provides a structure for analyzing transactions. After all transactions have been analyzed, the financial statements—income statement, statement of owner's equity, and balance sheet—are prepared. Let's look at each of these learning objectives in detail.

Objective 1.   Define the accounting elements.

Accounting elements are the parts that make up the accounting equation: assets, liabilities, and owner's equity. **Assets** are items *owned* by the business that will provide future benefits. **Liabilities** are debts *owed* by the business and will require a future outflow of assets. **Owner's equity** (also called net worth or capital) is the difference between assets and liabilities. **Revenues** represent the amount a business charges customers for products sold or services provided. Revenues create an inflow of assets. **Expenses** represent an outflow of assets (or increase in liabilities) as a result of the efforts made to generate revenues.

Objective 2.   Construct the accounting equation.

The accounting equation shows the relationship among assets, liabilities, and owner's equity (the accounting elements).

$$\text{Assets} = \text{Liabilities} + \text{Owner's Equity}$$

When given two of the numbers for the equation above, you can calculate the missing number by adding or subtracting.

The accounting equation may be expanded to include revenues, expenses, and drawing. Although drawing is not considered a major element in the accounting equation, it is a very special type of owner's equity account. It represents the withdrawals of assets from the business by the owner.

ASSETS (Items Owned)			LIABILITIES (Amts. Owed)		OWNER'S EQUITY				
					(Owner's Investment)		(Earnings)		
Cash	+	Delivery Equipment	= Accounts Payable	+	Rohan Macsen, Capital	− Rohan Macsen, Drawing	+ Revenues	− Expenses

Objective 3.   Analyze business transactions.

Analyzing is the first step in the accounting process. Three questions must be answered: (1) What happened? (2) Which accounts are affected, and what kind of accounts are they (asset, liability, owner's equity)? (3) How is the accounting equation affected? (Accounts will increase or decrease, but the equation always remains in balance.)

Objective 4.   Show the effects of business transactions on the accounting equation.

Each transaction will affect asset, liability, owner's equity, revenue, or expense accounts. For example, when an owner invests cash in the business, the asset account called *Cash* increases, and the owner's equity account *Capital* also increases.

For each transaction, you must decide what accounts are affected and whether the accounts increase or decrease. After each transaction, the equation must still be in balance.

Objective 5.   Prepare and describe the purposes of a simple income statement, statement of owner's equity, and balance sheet.

After the transactions are completed, the financial statements are prepared to show the results of those transactions. As shown on page 7, all financial statements have a heading that indicates the name of the firm, title of the statement, and time period or date covered by the statement. The income statement reports revenues, expenses, and the net income for the period. The statement of owner's equity shows the beginning balance of the owner's capital account, plus investments and net income, less withdrawals to compute the ending capital balance. The balance sheet reports all assets, liabilities, and the owner's capital on a certain date and confirms that the accounting equation has remained in balance.

Note that net income computed on the income statement is transferred to the statement of owner's equity to compute Patty V's capital at the end of the month. Patty V's capital on December 31, 20--, is then transferred to the balance sheet to compute total liabilities and owner's equity.

Objective 6.   Define the three basic phases of the accounting process.

The three basic phases of the accounting process are input, processing, and output. The inputs to the accounting process are the business transactions. These transactions are processed to recognize their effects on the assets, liabilities, owner's equity, revenues, and expenses of the business. The results of these events are then reported as outputs of the accounting process in the financial statements.

Patty V's Consulting Income Statement For Month Ended December 31, 20--		
Revenues		
Consulting fees		$10,000
Expenses		
Wages expense	$5,000	
Rent expense	1,500	
Phone expense	500	
Total expenses		7,000
Net income		$ 3,000

Patty V's Consulting Statement of Owner's Equity For Month Ended December 31, 20--		
Patty V, capital, December 1, 20--		$ ——
Investment in December		20,000
Total investment		$20,000
Net income for December	$3,000	
Less withdrawals for December	1,000	
Increase in capital		2,000
Patty V, capital, December 31, 20--		$22,000

Patty V's Consulting Balance Sheet December 31, 20--			
Assets		Liabilities	
Cash	$ 500	Accounts payable	$ 6,500
Accounts receivable	8,000		
Computer equipment	20,000	Owner's Equity	
		Patty V, capital	22,000
		Total liabilities and	
Total assets	$28,500	owner's equity	$28,500

REVIEW QUESTIONS

Instructions: Analyze each of the following items carefully before writing your answer in the column at the right.

Question	Answer

LO 2   1.   The entire accounting process is based on one simple equation called the _____. ....

LO 1   2.   An individual, association, or organization that engages in business activities is called a(n) _____. ....

LO 1   3.   An item owned by a business that will provide future benefits is a(n) _____. ....

LO 1   4.   Something owed to another business entity is a(n) _____. ....

LO 1   5.   A(n) _____ is an unwritten promise to pay a supplier for assets purchased or a service rendered. ....

LO 2   6.   The amount by which assets exceed the liabilities of a business is called _____. ....

LO 1   7.   According to the _____ concept, nonbusiness assets and liabilities are not included in the business entity's records. ....

LO 2   8.   Assets – Liabilities = _____. ....

LO 2   9.   Assets – Owner's Equity = _____. ....

LO 2 10.   Assets = Liabilities + _____. ....

LO 4 11.   The outflow of assets (or increase in liabilities) as the result of efforts to produce revenue is called a(n) _____. ....

LO 4 12.   When total revenues exceed total expenses, the difference is called _____. ....

LO 4 13.   When expenses are greater than revenues, the difference is called _____. ....

LO 4 14.   Any accounting period of 12 months' duration is called a(n) _____. ....

LO 4 15.   Withdrawals, or _____, represent a reduction in owner's equity because the owner takes cash or other assets for personal use. ....

LO 5 16.   The financial statement that reports the profitability of the business for a period of time is the _____. ....

LO 5 17.   The financial statement that shows investments and withdrawals by the owner, as well as profit or loss generated by the business, is the _____. ....

LO 5 18.   The financial statement that reports the assets, liabilities, and owner's equity on a specific date is the _____. ....

LO 5 19. On the balance sheet, assets are listed in order of _____, or the
ease with which they can be converted to cash. .... _____

EXERCISES

Exercise 1 (LO 2) THE ACCOUNTING EQUATION

Using the accounting equation provided below, compute the missing amounts.

	ASSETS	=	LIABILITIES	+	OWNER'S EQUITY
(a)	_____	=	$4,000	+	$20,000
(b)	$25,000	=	$8,000	+	_____
(c)	$50,000	=	_____	+	$10,000

Exercise 2 (LO 2/4) THE EXPANDED ACCOUNTING EQUATION

Using the accounting equation provided below, compute the missing amounts.

	ASSETS (Items Owned)	=	LIABILITIES (Amts. Owed)	+	OWNER'S EQUITY					
					(Owner's Investment)			(Earnings)		
	Cash		Accounts Payable		Capital	− Drawing	+	Revenues	−	Expenses
(a)	_____	=	$60,000	+	$20,000	− $10,000	+	$80,000	−	$60,000
(b)	$80,000	=	_____	+	$35,000	− $ 5,000	+	$70,000	−	$55,000
(c)	$90,000	=	$25,000	+	_____	− $ 2,000	+	$57,000	−	$50,000
(d)	$60,000	=	$20,000	+	$30,000	− $ 5,000	+	_____	−	$40,000
(e)	$40,000	=	$25,000	+	$40,000	− $ 5,000	+	$30,000	−	_____
(f)	$75,000	=	$20,000	+	$50,000	− _____	+	$40,000	−	$25,000

Exercise 3 (LO 5) STATEMENT OF OWNER'S EQUITY

If owner's equity was $38,000 at the beginning of the period and $45,000 at the end of the period, compute the net income or loss for the period. (There were no investments or withdrawals during the period.)

Exercise 4 (LO 2) ACCOUNTING EQUATION

If Irma Elkton, a dentist, owns office equipment amounting to $3,500, laboratory equipment amounting to $10,000, and other property that is used in the business amounting to $4,620, and owes business suppliers a total of $5,000, what is the owner's equity in the business?

Exercise 5 (LO 2) ACCOUNTING EQUATION

This is an extension of Exercise 4. One year later, the amount of Dr. Elkton's business assets has increased to a total of $22,000, and the amount of business liabilities has increased to a total of $6,000. Assuming that Dr. Elkton has not made any additional investments or withdrawals, compute the following:

(a) Owner's equity at year-end $ _____

(b) Net income or loss for the year $ _____

Exercise 6 (LO 3/4) EFFECTS OF TRANSACTIONS (BALANCE SHEET ACCOUNTS)

Rich Brite has started his own business. During the first month, the following transactions occurred:

(a) Invested $15,000 cash in the business, which was used to open a bank account.
(b) Purchased office equipment for cash, $4,000.
(c) Purchased a computer on account for $9,000.
(d) Paid $2,000 on account for the computer.

Using the lines provided below, show the effect of each transaction on the basic elements of the accounting equation: assets, liabilities, and owner's equity. Compute the new amounts for each element after each transaction to satisfy yourself that the accounting equation has remained in balance.

	ASSETS	=	LIABILITIES	+	OWNER'S EQUITY
(a)	_____		_____		_____
Bal.	_____		_____		_____
(b)	_____		_____		_____
	_____		_____		_____
Bal.	_____		_____		_____
(c)	_____		_____		_____
Bal.	_____		_____		_____
(d)	_____		_____		_____
Bal.	_____		_____		_____

Exercise 7 (LO 3/4) EFFECTS OF TRANSACTIONS (REVENUE, EXPENSE, WITHDRAWALS)

In late May, Glen Ross opened a business by investing $20,000 cash and purchasing office equipment on account for $8,000. These events were properly entered in the accounting records. In June, the following transactions took place:

(a) Received $4,000 from a client for professional services rendered.
(b) Paid $1,200 office rent for the month.
(c) Paid $200 to the power company for the month's utility bill.
(d) Withdrew $600 cash for personal use.

On the first Balance (Bal.) line provided on the following page, record the amount of assets, liabilities, and owner's equity as the result of Ross's investment and purchase of office equipment in May. Then, record the effect of transactions (a) to (d) on the expanded accounting equation: Assets = Liabilities + Owner's Equity (Capital – Drawing + Revenues – Expenses). Following transaction (d), compute the new balances for each category to satisfy yourself that the accounting equation has remained in balance.

Exercise 7 (Concluded)

	ASSETS (Items Owned)	= LIABILITIES + (Amts. Owed)	OWNER'S EQUITY (Owner's Investment)		(Earnings)			
	Cash	Accounts Payable	Glen Ross, Capital	− Glen Ross, Drawing	+ Revenues	− Expenses	Description	
Bal.	_____	_____	_____	_____	_____	_____	_____	
(a)	_____	_____	_____	_____	_____	_____	_____	
(b)	_____	_____	_____	_____	_____	_____	_____	
(c)	_____	_____	_____	_____	_____	_____	_____	
(d)	_____	_____	_____	_____	_____	_____	_____	
Bal.	======	======	======	======	======	======	======	

Exercise 8 (LO 3/4) EFFECTS OF TRANSACTIONS (ALL ACCOUNTS)

Judith Moore started her own business. During the month of July, the following transactions occurred:

(a) Invested $10,000 cash in the business.
(b) Purchased office equipment for $5,500 on account.
(c) Received $900 cash from a client for services rendered.
(d) Purchased computer equipment for cash, $6,000.
(e) Received $1,500 cash from a client for services rendered.
(f) Paid $800 office rent for the month.
(g) Paid the phone bill for the month, $75.
(h) Paid $100 on account, for office equipment previously purchased.
(i) Withdrew $500 for personal use.

Required:

1. Record the effect of each of the transactions listed above on the accounting equation provided in the chart on the following page. Following transaction (i), compute the new balances for the accounts to satisfy yourself that the equation has remained in balance.

Exercise 8 (Concluded)

	Cash	Office + Equipment =	Accounts Payable	J. Moore, + Capital –	J. Moore, Drawing +	Revenues –	Expenses	Description
	ASSETS (Items Owned)		= LIABILITIES + (Amts. Owed)	OWNER'S EQUITY (Owner's Investment)		(Earnings)		
(a)								
(b)								
(c)								
(d)								
(e)								
(f)								
(g)								
(h)								
(i)								
Bal.								

2. After recording the transactions in part (1), compute the following:

Total assets .... $ _____

Total liabilities .... $ _____

Owner's equity .... $ _____

Owner's equity in excess of original investment .... $ _____

Total revenues .... $ _____

Total expenses .... $ _____

Net income .... $ _____

Exercise 9 (LO 5) PREPARATION OF AN INCOME STATEMENT

Based on the transactions reported in Exercise 8, prepare an income statement for Judith Moore Enterprises for the month ended July 31, 20--, in the space provided below.

Exercise 10 (LO 5) PREPARATION OF THE STATEMENT OF OWNER'S EQUITY

Based on the transactions reported in Exercise 8, prepare a statement of owner's equity for Judith Moore Enterprises for the month ended July 31, 20--, in the space provided below.

Exercise 11 (LO 5) PREPARATION OF A BALANCE SHEET

Based on the transactions reported in Exercise 8, prepare a balance sheet as of July 31, 20--, in the space provided below.

PROBLEMS

Problem 12 (LO 2) THE ACCOUNTING EQUATION

Dr. Abe Miller is a general practitioner. As of December 31, Miller owned the following assets related to the professional practice:

Cash	$3,300	X-ray equipment	$7,000
Office equipment	4,500	Laboratory equipment	4,000

As of that date, Miller owed business suppliers as follows:

General Office Equipment Inc.	$2,000
Young Medical Supply Company	1,500
Buck Gas Company	1,200

Required:

1. Compute the amount of assets, liabilities, and owner's equity as of December 31.

    ASSETS   =   LIABILITIES   +   OWNER'S EQUITY

    _____   _____   _____

2. Assuming that during January there is an increase of $4,600 in Dr. Miller's business assets and an increase of $2,500 in business liabilities, compute the resulting accounting equation as of January 31.

    ASSETS   =   LIABILITIES   +   OWNER'S EQUITY

    _____   _____   _____

3. Assuming that during February there is a decrease of $1,500 in assets and a decrease of $1,200 in liabilities, compute the resulting accounting equation as of February 28.

    ASSETS   =   LIABILITIES   +   OWNER'S EQUITY

    _____   _____   _____

4. Assuming that Dr. Miller made no additional investments or withdrawals, compute the net income or loss for each month.

Problem 13 (LO 3/4) EFFECT OF TRANSACTIONS ON ACCOUNTING EQUATION

Susan Cole started her own consulting business in October 20--. During the first month, the following transactions occurred:

(a) Invested $12,000 cash in the business.
(b) Purchased office equipment for $7,500 on account.
(c) Purchased computer equipment for cash, $800.
(d) Received $700 cash from a client for services rendered.
(e) Paid $600 office rent for the month.
(f) Paid student assistant wages for the month, $150.
(g) Paid one-year insurance premium, $200.
(h) Paid $3,000 on account for the office equipment purchased in transaction (b).
(i) Withdrew cash for personal use, $100.

Problem 13 (Concluded)

Required:

1. Record the effect of each of the transactions from the previous page on the accounting equation chart provided below. Following transaction (i), compute the new amounts in the accounts.

	ASSETS			= LIABILITIES +		OWNER'S EQUITY				
				(Amts. Owed)	(Owner's Investment)		(Earnings)			
	(Items Owned)									
	Cash +	Office Equip. +	Prepaid Insur. =	Accounts Payable +	S. Cole, Capital −	S. Cole, Drawing +	Revenues −	Expenses	Description
(a)									
(b)									
(c)									
(d)									
(e)									
(f)									
(g)									
(h)									
(i)									
Bal.									

2. After recording the transactions, compute the following:

Total assets .... $ _____

Total liabilities .... $ _____

Owner's equity .... $ _____

Change in owner's equity from original investment .... $ _____

Total revenues .... $ _____

Total expenses .... $ _____

Net income (loss) .... $ _____

Problem 14 (LO 5) INCOME STATEMENT

Based on the transactions in Problem 13, prepare an income statement for Susan Cole Consulting Services for the month ended October 31, 20--, in the space provided below.

Problem 15 (LO 5) STATEMENT OF OWNER'S EQUITY

Based on the transactions in Problem 13, prepare a statement of owner's equity for Susan Cole Consulting Services for the month ended October 31, 20--, in the space provided below.

Problem 16 (LO 5) BALANCE SHEET

Based on the transactions in Problem 13, prepare a balance sheet as of October 31, 20--, in the space provided below.

Problem 17 (LO 3/4/5) ANALYZE THE EFFECTS OF BUSINESS TRANSACTIONS ON THE ACCOUNTING EQUATION AND PREPARE FINANCIAL STATEMENTS

Stuart Cassady is opening a typing service. During the first month (April 20--), the following transactions occurred:

(a) Invested $10,000 in the business.

(b) Purchased office supplies for $200 cash.

(c) Purchased office supplies for $800, $400 on account and $400 in cash.

(d) Received typing fees of $300 cash.

(e) Paid the rent, $600.

(f) Withdrew $100 for personal use.

(g) Earned typing fees of $600, $200 in cash and $400 on account.

(h) Made partial payment for office supplies in transaction (c) of $200.

(i) Received $200 cash for typing fees earned on account in transaction (g).

Required:

1. Record the effect of each transaction on the accounting equation below. Following transaction (i), compute new amounts for each account.

	Cash	Accounts + Receivable. +	Office Supplies =	Accounts Payable +	S. Cassady, Capital −	S. Cassady, Drawing +	Revenues −	Expenses	Description
(a)									
(b)									
(c)									
(d)									
(e)									
(f)									
(g)									
(h)									
(i)									
Bal.									

ASSETS (Items Owned) = LIABILITIES + (Amts. Owed) OWNER'S EQUITY (Owner's Investment) (Earnings)

Problem 17 (Concluded)

2. Based on the transactions in part (1) of Problem 17, prepare an income statement, statement of owner's equity, and balance sheet for Stuart Cassady Typing Service.

Income Statement

Statement of Owner's Equity

Balance Sheet

CHAPTER 3
THE DOUBLE-ENTRY FRAMEWORK

LEARNING OBJECTIVES

Objective 1.   Define the parts of a T account.

The **T account** gets its name from the fact that it resembles the letter *T*. There are three major parts of an account. The title of the account is on top. The left side of the T account is the debit side, and the right side is the credit side.

Objective 2.   Foot and balance a T account.

To determine the balance of a T account, simply total the dollar amounts of the debit and credit sides. These totals are known as **footings.** The difference between the footings is called the *balance* of the account. The balance is written on the side with the larger footing.

Objective 3.   Describe the effects of debits and credits on specific types of accounts.

Assets are on the left side of the accounting equation. Thus, increases are entered on the left, or debit, side; and decreases are entered on the right, or credit, side. The normal balance of an asset account is a debit.

Liabilities and owner's equity are on the right side of the equation. Thus, increases are entered on the right, or credit, side; and decreases are entered on the left, or debit, side. The normal balance of a liability and owner's capital account is a credit.

Revenues increase owner's equity. Thus, increases in revenue are recorded as credits. The normal balance of a revenue account is a credit.

Expenses decrease owner's equity. Thus, increases in expenses are recorded as debits. The normal balance of an expense account is a debit.

Withdrawals of cash and other assets by the owner for personal reasons decrease owner's equity. Thus, an increase in drawing is recorded as a debit. The normal balance of a drawing account is a debit.

The following figure should be helpful in developing your understanding of debits and credits and the accounting equation:

Assets		=	Liabilities		+	Owner's Equity	
Debit +	Credit −		Debit −	Credit +		Debit −	Credit +

Rohan Macsen, Capital	
Debit −	Credit +

Expenses		Revenues	
Debit +	Credit −	Debit −	Credit +

Drawing	
Debit +	Credit −

Objective 4.   Use T accounts to analyze transactions.

There are three basic questions that must be answered when analyzing a transaction: (1) What happened? (2) Which accounts are affected? and (3) How is the accounting equation affected? After analyzing the transaction, in every instance, debits will equal credits.

Objective 5.   Prepare a trial balance and explain its purposes and linkages with the financial statements.

There are two very important rules in double-entry accounting: (1) The sum of the debits must equal the sum of the credits. This means that at least two accounts are affected by each transaction. (2) The accounting equation must remain in balance.

A **trial balance** is a list of all accounts showing the title and balance of each account. The total debits and credits must be equal. A trial balance is not a formal statement or report. It can be used as an aid in preparing the financial statements.

REVIEW QUESTIONS

Instructions: Analyze each of the following items carefully before writing your answer in the column at the right.

	Question	**Answer**

LO 1   1.   A form or record used to keep track of the increases and decreases in each type of asset, liability, owner's equity, revenue, and expense is known as a(n) _____. .... _____

LO 1   2.   The left side of a T account is called the _____ side. .... _____

LO 1   3.   The right side of a T account is called the _____ side. .... _____

LO 2   4.   The process of entering totals in the debit and credit sides of a T account is referred to as _____. .... _____

LO 2   5.   The amount of the difference between the debits and credits recorded in a T account is called the _____. .... _____

LO 3   6.   An increase in the asset Cash is recorded by a(n) _____. .... _____

LO 3   7.   An increase in the liability Accounts Payable is recorded by a(n) _____. .... _____

LO 3   8.   The normal balance of a revenue account is on the _____ side. ... _____

LO 3   9.   A decrease in the liability Accounts Payable is recorded by a(n) _____. .... _____

LO 3   10.   The normal balance of a liability account is on the _____ side. ... _____

LO 4   11.   The fact that each transaction has a dual effect on the accounting elements provides the basis for what is called _____. .... _____

LO 5   12.   A list of all of the accounts showing the title and balance of each account is called the _____. .... _____

EXERCISES

Exercise 1 (LO 1) DEFINING PARTS OF THE T ACCOUNT

Provided below are T accounts for the six types of accounts discussed to this point. Identify the debit and credit side of each type of account by writing debit on the debit side and credit on the credit side.

Assets	Liabilities	Owner's Capital	Owner's Drawing	Expenses	Revenues

Exercise 2 (LO 3) EFFECTS OF DEBITS AND CREDITS

Indicate whether each of the following types of accounts would normally have a debit or credit balance by circling either debit or credit in the column at the right:

Type of Account	Normal Balance (Circle one)	
(a) Assets..	Debit	Credit
(b) Liabilities...	Debit	Credit
(c) Owner's capital..	Debit	Credit
(d) Revenues	Debit	Credit
(e) Expenses..	Debit	Credit
(f) Drawing...	Debit	Credit

Exercise 3 (LO 3) INCREASING AND DECREASING ACCOUNTS WITH DEBITS AND CREDITS

Provided below are T accounts representing the six types of accounts discussed. Indicate how each account would be increased and decreased by placing a (+) or (–) on the debit and credit side of each account.

Assets	Liabilities	Owner's Capital	Owner's Drawing	Expenses	Revenues

Exercise 4 (LO 4) USING T ACCOUNTS TO ANALYZE TRANSACTIONS

The following transactions were completed by Jacque Hamon, an educational consultant. Analyze each transaction and enter the amounts in the proper debit and credit positions in the T accounts at the right.

(a) Invested $3,000 cash in the business.

Cash   Jacque Hamon, Capital

(b) Received $1,000 in cash for consulting services rendered.

Cash   Professional Fees

(c) Bought office equipment from Gusse Supply Co. on account, $500.

Office Equipment   Accounts Payable

(d) Paid electric bill, $75.

Cash   Utilities Expense

Exercise 4 (Concluded)

(e)   Paid Gusse Supply $200 on account.

Cash		Accounts Payable

(f)   Received $300 in cash for consulting services
rendered.

Cash		Professional Fees

(g)   Borrowed $1,000 from bank by signing a note.

Cash		Notes Payable

(h)   Paid the phone bill, $50.

Cash		Phone Expense

Exercise 5 (LO 4) USING T ACCOUNTS TO ANALYZE TRANSACTIONS (BALANCE SHEET ACCOUNTS)

Connie Sung has started her own typing business. During the first month, the following transactions occurred:

(a)   Invested $12,000 cash in the business, and the money was deposited in a bank account.
(b)   Purchased a new computer and printer on account from Stahl Electronics for $8,000.
(c)   Paid the premium on a one-year insurance policy on computer equipment, $75 cash.
(d)   Secured a bank loan by signing a note for $5,000.
(e)   Made payment of $3,000 to Stahl Electronics on account.

Required:

Record the above transactions in the T accounts provided below.

Assets		=	Liabilities			Owner's Equity	
Debit +	Credit –		Debit –	Credit +		Debit –	Credit +

Cash		Accounts Payable		C. Sung, Capital	

Office Equipment		Notes Payable	

Prepaid Insurance	

Exercise 6 (LO 4) USING T ACCOUNTS TO ANALYZE TRANSACTIONS (ALL ACCOUNTS)

In late April, Frazier Baar opened a psychiatry practice by investing $9,000 cash and purchasing a couch, chair, and leather-covered note pad on account for $2,500. These events were properly entered in the accounting records. In May, Dr. Baar began seeing patients and entered into the following transactions:

(a) Received $500 for counseling services rendered.
(b) Paid $100 for *Psychology Today* and other magazines for patients to read in the waiting room.
(c) Paid $1,200 office rent for the month.

Required:

1. Enter the balances as of May 1 in the following accounts: Cash, Office Furnishings, Accounts Payable, and F. Baar, Capital.

2. Record the May transactions in the accounts listed below.

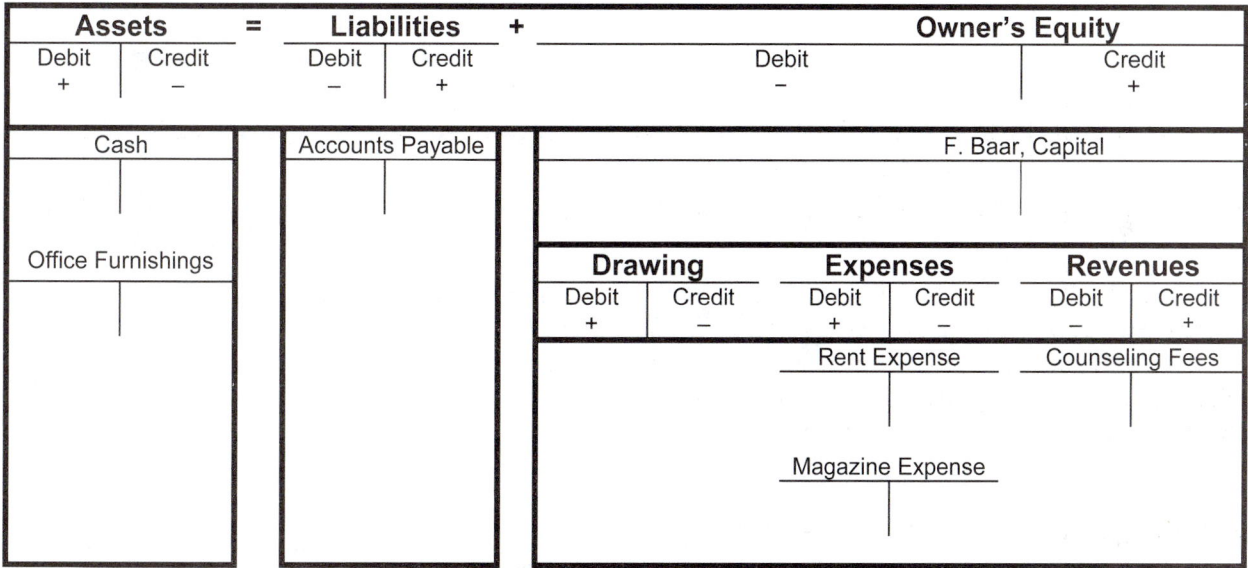

Exercise 7 (LO 2/4) USING T ACCOUNTS TO ANALYZE TRANSACTIONS, FOOTING AND BALANCING T ACCOUNTS

In January 20--, Blanca Estavez, CPA, started her own accounting practice. The following is a list of transactions for the first month:

(a) Invested $20,000 cash in the business.
(b) Purchased office supplies, $500 cash.
(c) Purchased office furniture, $6,000 cash.
(d) Purchased a computer and printer for $9,000: $5,000 cash and $4,000 on account.
(e) Paid $800 for accounting software programs.
(f) Performed accounting services and earned fees totaling $1,800: $1,200 in cash and $600 on account.
(g) Paid $700 rent for the month.
(h) Withdrew $200 for personal use.
(i) Paid $2,000 on account for the computer.

Exercise 7 (Concluded)

Required:

1. Record the transactions in the T accounts that follow.
2. After all transactions have been entered, foot and balance the T accounts.

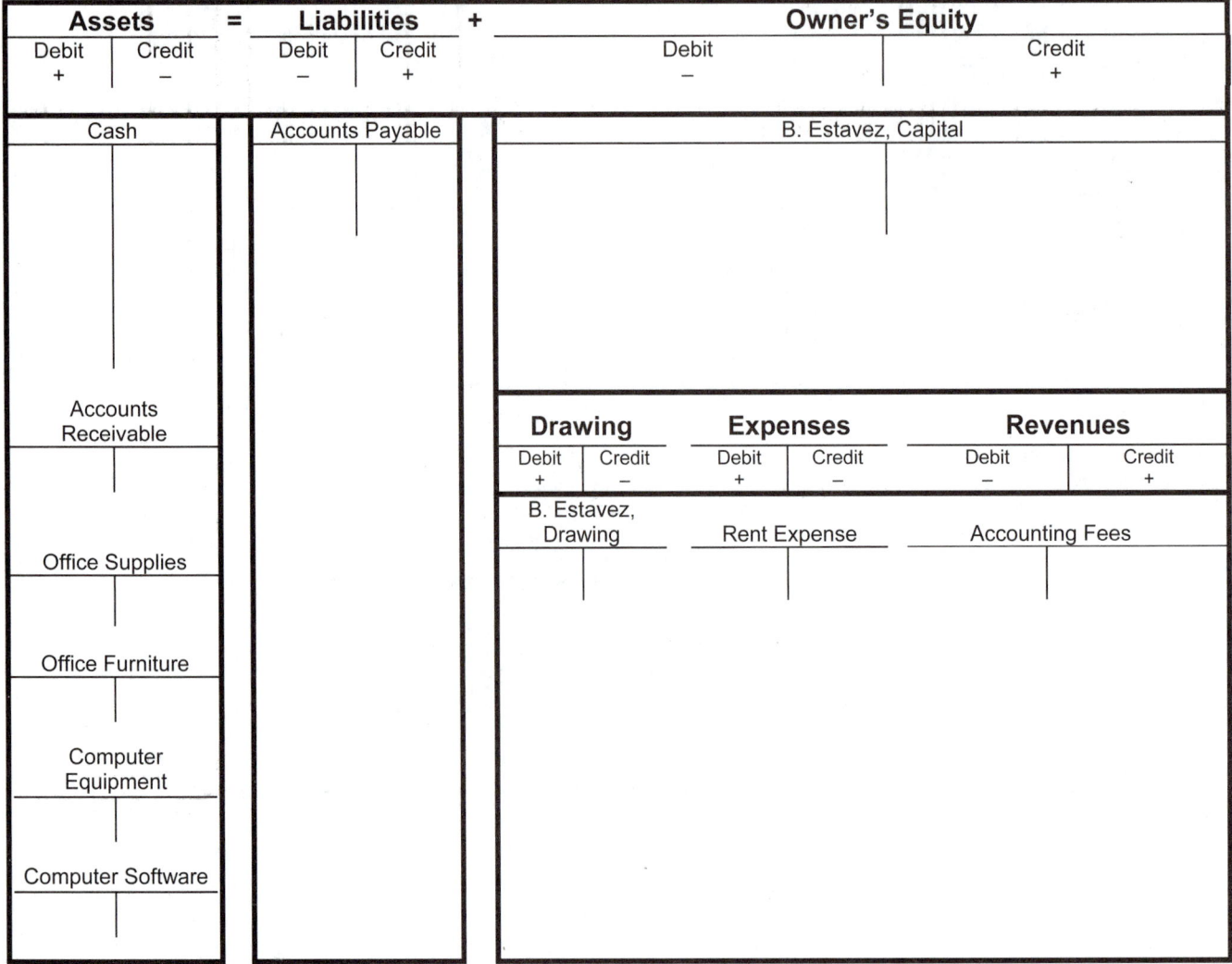

Exercise 8 (LO 5) PREPARE A TRIAL BALANCE

Based on the transactions recorded in Exercise 7, prepare a trial balance at the end of the first month of operations using the form provided below.

ACCOUNT	DEBIT BALANCE	CREDIT BALANCE

PROBLEMS

Problem 9 (LO 2/4/5) ANALYZING TRANSACTIONS WITH T ACCOUNTS, FOOTING AND BALANCING ACCOUNTS, AND PREPARING A TRIAL BALANCE

Jali Abdul has decided to offer his services as a promoter for local rock-n-roll bands. Following is a narrative of selected transactions completed during January, the first month of J. A. Productions' operations:
(a) Invested $10,000 in the business and opened a checking account.
(b) Purchased office furniture on account at a cost of $5,000.
(c) Purchased computer equipment for $4,500. Abdul paid $1,500 cash and promised to pay the balance over the next three months.
(d) Purchased office supplies for cash, $350.
(e) Sent letters to numerous performing groups throughout the region explaining the services available through J. A. Productions. Postage of $200 was paid in cash.
(f) Began arranging performances throughout the region after securing contracts with several groups. The phone bill came to $300 and was paid in cash.
(g) Earned promotion revenue of $2,500: $2,000 in cash and $500 on account.
(h) Paid part-time receptionist $600.
(i) Withdrew $1,000 for personal use.
(j) Paid $2,500 on account for the office furniture purchased in part (b).
(k) Collected $250 for promotional fees earned on account.

Problem 9 (Continued)

Required:

1. Record the transactions in the T accounts provided.
2. Foot and balance the accounts.
3. Prepare a trial balance of the accounts as of January 31, 20--, using the form provided.

1. and 2.

Assets	=	Liabilities	+	Owner's Equity	
Debit +	Credit −	Debit −	Credit +	Debit −	Credit +

Cash

Accounts Payable

J. Abdul, Capital

Accounts Receivable

Drawing		Expenses		Revenues	
Debit +	Credit −	Debit +	Credit −	Debit −	Credit +

Office Supplies

J. Abdul, Drawing

Wages Expense

Promotion Fees

Office Furniture

Phone Expense

Computer Equipment

Postage Expense

Problem 9 (Concluded)

3. _____

_____

ACCOUNT	DEBIT BALANCE	CREDIT BALANCE

Problem 10 (LO 5) REVIEW: ACCOUNTING EQUATION AND FINANCIAL STATEMENTS

Based on the transactions recorded in Problem 9, select the information needed to fill in the blank space in the following statements:

(a)   Total revenue for the month   _____

(b)   Total expenses for the month   _____

(c)   Net income for the month   _____

(d)   Abdul's original investment in the business   _____

    + Net income for the month   _____

    − Owner's drawing   _____

    Increase in capital   _____

    = Owner's equity at the end of the month   _____

(e)   End-of-month accounting equation:

Assets	=	Liabilities	+	Owner's Equity
_____		_____		_____

Problem 11 (LO 5) REVIEW: PREPARATION OF FINANCIAL STATEMENTS

Refer to the trial balance in Problem 9 and to the analysis of the change in owner's equity in Problem 10.

(a)   Prepare an income statement for J. A. Productions for the month ended January 31, 20--.

(b)   Prepare a statement of owner's equity for J. A. Productions for the month ended January 31, 20--.

(c)   Prepare a balance sheet for J. A. Productions as of January 31, 20--.

(a)

Problem 11 (Concluded)

(b) _____

(c) _____

CHAPTER 4
JOURNALIZING AND POSTING TRANSACTIONS

LEARNING OBJECTIVES

Chapter 3 introduced the double-entry framework and illustrated the impact of debits and credits on the accounting equation and T accounts. In Chapter 4, business transactions are entered into the general journal and posted to general ledger accounts.

Objective 1.   Describe the flow of data from source documents to the trial balance.

The flow of financial data from the source documents through the accounting information systems follows the steps listed below.

1.   Analyze what happened by using information from source documents and the firm's chart of accounts.
2.   Enter business transactions in the general journal.
3.   Post entries to accounts in the general ledger.
4.   Prepare a trial balance.

INPUT   PROCESSING

Objective 2.   Describe and explain the purpose of source documents.

A **source document** provides objective information needed to record a transaction. Examples include check stubs, receipts, cash register tapes, sales invoices, and memos. Source documents are analyzed to determine which accounts should be increased or decreased.

Objective 3.   Describe the chart of accounts as a means of classifying financial information.

The **chart of accounts** lists in numerical order all of the accounts being used by a business. Assets are listed first (begin with "1"); liabilities are second (begin with "2"); owner's equity accounts are third (begin with "3"); revenues are fourth (begin with "4"); and expenses are last (begin with "5"). In a three-digit account numbering system, for example, Cash may be account number 101 and Accounts Receivable may be account number 122. Spacing numbers this way permits easy addition of new accounts as the business grows.

Objective 4.   Journalize transactions.

Journalizing is the process of entering information into the journal, or book of original entry. This simply means the journal is the first place a transaction is recorded. The general journal has space to enter the date of the transaction, the name of the accounts being debited and credited, the account numbers, and the amounts of the debits and credits. A brief description follows each journal entry stating the reason for the entry.

Objective 5.   Post to the general ledger and prepare a trial balance.

Once the transactions are entered into the general journal, they must be **posted** to (copied to) the individual accounts, which are located in the general ledger. The accounts are in the general ledger in the chart of accounts order. That is, the assets are first, followed by liabilities, owner's equity, revenue, and expense accounts.

In this chapter, the general ledger accounts are in the form of four-column accounts. This is better than the T account because a running balance is maintained.

The **trial balance** is a listing of account balances at the end of the month—after all the transactions have been posted from the general journal to the general ledger accounts. The total of the debit balances must equal the total of the credit balances.

Objective 6.   Explain how to find and correct errors.

Finding errors can be a long and frustrating process. But there are some methods to reduce the time and effort needed. The first thing to do is double check your calculations and the accuracy of the posting activities. Common errors include sliding ($230 could become $23 or $2,300) and transposing numbers ($326 could become $236). Taking the difference between the debits and credits and dividing by 9 or by 2 may help locate the error.

There are two methods of correcting errors. The **ruling method** may be used before the transaction has been posted. Under this method, you draw a line through the incorrect title or amount and write in the correct information above the ruling. The **correcting entry method** is used after an entry has been posted to the general ledger. The correcting entry increases and decreases accounts in a manner that corrects the errors made in previous transactions.

REVIEW QUESTIONS

Instructions: Analyze each of the following items carefully before writing your answer in the column at the right.

	Question	**Answer**
LO 1/2 1.	A document that provides information about a business transaction is called a(n) _____.	_____
LO 3 2.	A list of all the accounts used by a business enterprise is called a(n) _____.	_____
LO 3 3.	Accounts that begin with the number "3" are _____.	_____
LO 3 4.	Expenses are accounts that begin with which number?	_____
LO 4 5.	A document that provides a day-by-day listing of transactions of a business is called a(n) _____.	_____
LO 4 6.	A journal is commonly referred to as a(n) _____ because it is here that the first formal accounting record is made.	_____
LO 4 7.	Transactions affecting more than two accounts are called _____. .	_____
LO 4 8.	The act of entering transactions into a journal is called _____. .	_____
LO 4 9.	In a journal, debits are entered first; then credits are entered and indented _____ (how much space).	_____
LO 5 10.	A complete set of all accounts used by a business is known as the _____.	_____

LO 5 11. A(n) _____ account allows the accountant to keep a running balance. .... _____

LO 5 12. The process of copying debits and credits from the journal to the ledger accounts is called _____. .... _____

LO 5 13. Posting from the journal to the ledger is done _____ or at frequent intervals. .... _____

LO 5 14. The information in the Posting Reference columns of the journal and the ledger accounts provides a link known as a(n) _____. .... _____

LO 5 15. A(n) _____ is taken after transactions are posted to the general ledger accounts to be sure that debit and credit balances in the ledger are equal. .... _____

LO 6 16. A(n) _____ error occurs when you move a number a decimal place to the right or left. .... _____

LO 6 17. A(n) _____ error occurs when you use the right numbers but in the wrong order. .... _____

LO 6 18. Drawing a line through the incorrect amount or account title and writing correct information above it is an example of the _____ method. .... _____

LO 6 19. When an incorrect entry has been journalized and posted, a(n) _____ entry is required. .... _____

EXERCISES

Exercise 1 (LO 4) REVIEW: TRANSACTION ANALYSIS

Before a transaction is recorded in the journal, it should be analyzed to determine the following:

(a)   What accounts are affected by the transaction.

(b)   Whether each affected account is to be increased or decreased.

(c)   Whether the increase or decrease is to be accomplished by a debit or credit.

In the following list of transactions for Abbott Service Co., indicate the names of the accounts to be debited and credited. Place a check mark in either the plus (+) or minus (−) column to indicate whether the account has been increased or decreased. The first transaction is entered as an illustration.

Transaction		Account	(+)	(−)
1. J. A. Abbott invested cash in a business enterprise.	Debit:	Cash	✓	
	Credit:	J. A. Abbott, Capital	✓	
2. Received cash for services provided.	Debit:	_____	____	____
	Credit:	_____	____	____

Transaction		Account	(+)	(−)
3. Paid cash for rent on the office.	Debit:	_____	_____	_____
	Credit:	_____	_____	_____
4. Purchased office equipment on account.	Debit:	_____	_____	_____
	Credit	_____	_____	_____
5. Paid cash to a creditor for a debt previously owed.	Debit:	_____	_____	_____
	Credit:	_____	_____	_____
6. Paid the phone bill for the month.	Debit:	_____	_____	_____
	Credit:	_____	_____	_____
7. Paid supplier for office equipment purchased in transaction (4) above.	Debit:	_____	_____	_____
	Credit:	_____	_____	_____
8. Paid cash for a car for the owner's personal use.	Debit:	_____	_____	_____
	Credit:	_____	_____	_____
9. Paid temporary secretary's wages.	Debit:	_____	_____	_____
	Credit:	_____	_____	_____
10. Performed services that will be paid for later.	Debit:	_____	_____	_____
	Credit:	_____	_____	_____

Exercise 2 (LO 4) JOURNALIZING TRANSACTIONS

Susan Poe started a business, Poe's Connections. She provides resource referral services whereby she helps businesses locate vendors of specialty products and vice versa. She charges a referral fee to her clients who may be businesses or vendors. She has a part-time clerk who enters information into a database to match requests with potential users or suppliers. Her chart of accounts is as follows:

Assets
   101 Cash
   122 Accounts Receivable
   182 Office Furniture

Liabilities
   202 Accounts Payable

Owner's Equity
   311 Susan Poe, Capital
   312 Susan Poe, Drawing

Revenues
   401 Referral Fees

Expenses
   511 Wages Expense
   521 Rent Expense

Exercise 2 (Continued)

Required:

Enter the following transactions in the two-column journal provided on the next page.

20--

May	1	Susan invested $5,000 cash to start the business.
	5	Purchased office furniture on account, $3,000.
	9	Paid office rent for the month, $450.
	10	Received fees for referral services, $500.
	15	Made payment on account (for office furniture), $100.
	20	Earned referral fees: $125 cash and $175 on account.
	25	Paid wages to clerk for part-time work, $400.
	28	Withdrew cash for personal use, $100.
	29	Received cash for referral services previously rendered, $150.

Exercise 2 (Concluded)

GENERAL JOURNAL

	DATE		DESCRIPTION	POST. REF.	DEBIT	CREDIT	
1							1
2							2
3							3
4							4
5							5
6							6
7							7
8							8
9							9
10							10
11							11
12							12
13							13
14							14
15							15
16							16
17							17
18							18
19							19
20							20
21							21
22							22
23							23
24							24
25							25
26							26
27							27
28							28
29							29
30							30
31							31
32							32
33							33
34							34
35							35
36							36
37							37

Exercise 3 (LO 5) POST TO THE GENERAL LEDGER

Post the transactions from Exercise 2 to the general ledger accounts provided as follows. Be sure to enter the appropriate cross-reference information in the Posting Reference columns of the general ledger accounts and the general journal.

GENERAL LEDGER

ACCOUNT: Cash   ACCOUNT NO. 101

DATE	ITEM	POST. REF.	DEBIT	CREDIT	BALANCE DEBIT	BALANCE CREDIT

ACCOUNT: Accounts Receivable   ACCOUNT NO. 122

DATE	ITEM	POST. REF.	DEBIT	CREDIT	BALANCE DEBIT	BALANCE CREDIT

ACCOUNT: Office Furniture   ACCOUNT NO. 182

DATE	ITEM	POST. REF.	DEBIT	CREDIT	BALANCE DEBIT	BALANCE CREDIT

ACCOUNT: Accounts Payable   ACCOUNT NO. 202

DATE	ITEM	POST. REF.	DEBIT	CREDIT	BALANCE DEBIT	BALANCE CREDIT

Exercise 3 (Concluded)

GENERAL LEDGER

ACCOUNT: Susan Poe, Capital   ACCOUNT NO. 311

DATE	ITEM	POST. REF.	DEBIT	CREDIT	BALANCE DEBIT	BALANCE CREDIT

ACCOUNT: Susan Poe, Drawing   ACCOUNT NO. 312

DATE	ITEM	POST. REF.	DEBIT	CREDIT	BALANCE DEBIT	BALANCE CREDIT

ACCOUNT: Referral Fees   ACCOUNT NO. 401

DATE	ITEM	POST. REF.	DEBIT	CREDIT	BALANCE DEBIT	BALANCE CREDIT

ACCOUNT: Wages Expense   ACCOUNT NO. 511

DATE	ITEM	POST. REF.	DEBIT	CREDIT	BALANCE DEBIT	BALANCE CREDIT

ACCOUNT: Rent Expense   ACCOUNT NO. 521

DATE	ITEM	POST. REF.	DEBIT	CREDIT	BALANCE DEBIT	BALANCE CREDIT

Exercise 4 (LO 5) REVIEW: PREPARE A TRIAL BALANCE

After the transactions are posted in Exercise 3, prepare the trial balance.

ACCOUNT TITLE	ACCT. NO.	DEBIT BALANCE	CREDIT BALANCE

PROBLEMS

Problem 5 (LO 4/5) JOURNALIZING AND POSTING TRANSACTIONS FOLLOWED BY PREPARATION OF A TRIAL BALANCE

Della Jordan started her own business, D. J. Parties. For about $50 per hour, Della and a group of part-time associates serve as disc jockeys for parties held at the client's home. As part of the service, Della provides a lighting system, stereo equipment, CDs, and two disc jockeys working as a team for each party. A wide range of music is offered, and the client may provide additional CDs to be played. A chart of accounts is provided below.

D. J. Parties
Chart of Accounts

Assets			Owner's Equity		
101	Cash		311	Della Jordan, Capital	
122	Accounts Receivable		312	Della Jordan, Drawing	
181	Stereo Equipment				
182	Office Furniture		Revenue		
183	CDs		401	Disc Jockey Fees	
184	Lighting Equipment				
185	Van		Expenses		
			511	Wages Expense	
Liabilities			521	Rent Expense	
202	Accounts Payable		525	Phone Expense	
			538	Gas Expense	

Problem 5 (Continued)

The following transactions occurred during May, the first month of operation:

20--

May	1	Jordan invested $30,000 cash in the business. The funds were deposited in a business checking account.
	3	Purchased stereo equipment and speaker systems from Big Al's Discount Stereo for $7,000: $3,000 cash and $4,000 on account.
	4	Purchased compact discs and tapes for $2,500.
	4	Purchased lighting equipment for $2,000.
	5	Purchased office furniture on account, $500.
	7	Purchased a van to be used to haul the equipment to the clients' homes, $9,500.
	18	Earned fees for services rendered, $3,800: $800 cash and $3,000 on account.
	20	Paid part-time associates for work performed, $600.
	21	Made payment on account for stereo equipment bought on May 3, $1,500.
	25	Paid for gas for the van, $40.
	27	Paid phone bill, $80.
	28	Received cash for services previously rendered, $1,500.
	29	Paid part-time associates, $1,100.
	30	Paid rent, $500.
	30	Made payment on account for stereo equipment bought on May 3, $1,200.
	30	Jordan made withdrawal for personal use, $1,000.

Required:

1. Enter the transactions in the two-column journal provided on pages 45–46. Use journal page 1 for transactions through May 20. Enter the remainder on page 2.

2. Post the transactions from the journal to the general ledger accounts on pages 47–50.

3. Prepare a trial balance.

Problem 5 (Continued)

1. *[Instructor: Account numbers in Post. Ref. column are entered when completing requirement 2.]*

GENERAL JOURNAL

	DATE	DESCRIPTION	POST. REF.	DEBIT	CREDIT	
1						1
2						2
3						3
4						4
5						5
6						6
7						7
8						8
9						9
10						10
11						11
12						12
13						13
14						14
15						15
16						16
17						17
18						18
19						19
20						20
21						21
22						22
23						23
24						24
25						25
26						26
27						27
28						28
29						29
30						30
31						31
32						32
33						33

Problem 5 (Continued)

GENERAL JOURNAL

	DATE	DESCRIPTION	POST. REF.	DEBIT	CREDIT	
1						1
2						2
3						3
4						4
5						5
6						6
7						7
8						8
9						9
10						10
11						11
12						12
13						13
14						14
15						15
16						16
17						17
18						18
19						19
20						20
21						21
22						22
23						23
24						24
25						25
26						26
27						27
28						28
29						29
30						30
31						31
32						32
33						33

Problem 5 (Continued)
2.

GENERAL LEDGER

ACCOUNT: Cash   ACCOUNT NO.   101

DATE	ITEM	POST. REF.	DEBIT	CREDIT	BALANCE DEBIT	BALANCE CREDIT

ACCOUNT: Accounts Receivable   ACCOUNT NO.   122

DATE	ITEM	POST. REF.	DEBIT	CREDIT	BALANCE DEBIT	BALANCE CREDIT

ACCOUNT: Stereo Equipment   ACCOUNT NO.   181

DATE	ITEM	POST. REF.	DEBIT	CREDIT	BALANCE DEBIT	BALANCE CREDIT

Problem 5 (Continued)

ACCOUNT: Office Furniture   ACCOUNT NO.   182

DATE		ITEM	POST. REF.	DEBIT	CREDIT	BALANCE	
						DEBIT	CREDIT

ACCOUNT: CDs   ACCOUNT NO.   183

DATE		ITEM	POST. REF.	DEBIT	CREDIT	BALANCE	
						DEBIT	CREDIT

ACCOUNT: Lighting Equipment   ACCOUNT NO.   184

DATE		ITEM	POST. REF.	DEBIT	CREDIT	BALANCE	
						DEBIT	CREDIT

ACCOUNT: Van   ACCOUNT NO.   185

DATE		ITEM	POST. REF.	DEBIT	CREDIT	BALANCE	
						DEBIT	CREDIT

ACCOUNT: Accounts Payable   ACCOUNT NO.   202

DATE		ITEM	POST. REF.	DEBIT	CREDIT	BALANCE	
						DEBIT	CREDIT

Problem 5 (Continued)

ACCOUNT: Della Jordan, Capital   ACCOUNT NO.   311

DATE	ITEM	POST. REF.	DEBIT	CREDIT	BALANCE	
					DEBIT	CREDIT

ACCOUNT: Della Jordan, Drawing   ACCOUNT NO.   312

DATE	ITEM	POST. REF.	DEBIT	CREDIT	BALANCE	
					DEBIT	CREDIT

ACCOUNT: Disc Jockey Fees   ACCOUNT NO.   401

DATE	ITEM	POST. REF.	DEBIT	CREDIT	BALANCE	
					DEBIT	CREDIT

ACCOUNT: Wages Expense   ACCOUNT NO.   511

DATE	ITEM	POST. REF.	DEBIT	CREDIT	BALANCE	
					DEBIT	CREDIT

ACCOUNT: Rent Expense   ACCOUNT NO.   521

DATE	ITEM	POST. REF.	DEBIT	CREDIT	BALANCE	
					DEBIT	CREDIT

Problem 5 (Concluded)

ACCOUNT: Phone Expense   ACCOUNT NO.   525

DATE		ITEM	POST. REF.	DEBIT	CREDIT	BALANCE	
						DEBIT	CREDIT

ACCOUNT: Gas Expense   ACCOUNT NO.   538

DATE		ITEM	POST. REF.	DEBIT	CREDIT	BALANCE	
						DEBIT	CREDIT

3.

ACCOUNT TITLE	ACCT. NO.	DEBIT BALANCE	CREDIT BALANCE

Problem 6 (LO 5) REVIEW: PREPARATION OF FINANCIAL STATEMENTS

From the information in Problem 5, prepare an income statement, a statement of owner's equity, and a balance sheet.

Problem 6 (Concluded)

_____

_____

_____

Problem 7

1. (LO 6) CORRECTION OF ERRORS: The Ruling Method

The following journal entries were made but not posted. On January 1, $500 cash was withdrawn by the owner for personal use (R. J. Hammond) but was charged to Wages Expense. On January 2, $230 was paid on account. Make corrections using the ruling method.

GENERAL JOURNAL   PAGE

	DATE		DESCRIPTION	POST. REF.	DEBIT	CREDIT	
1	20-- Jan.	1	Wages Expense		5 0 0 00		1
2			Cash			5 0 0 00	2
3			Paid R. J. Hammond				3
4							4
5		2	Accounts Payable		3 2 0 00		5
6			Cash			3 2 0 00	6
7			Payment on account				7
8							8

Problem 7 (Concluded)

2. (LO 6) CORRECTION OF ERRORS: The Correcting Entry Method

On January 10, Office Equipment was debited for $800 when the debit should have been to Office Supplies. Since the entry has been posted, show the appropriate correcting entry made in the general journal on January 15.

GENERAL JOURNAL   PAGE

	DATE		DESCRIPTION	POST. REF.	DEBIT	CREDIT	
1							1
2							2
3							3
4							4
5							5
6							6
7							7
8							8

CHAPTER 5
ADJUSTING ENTRIES AND THE WORK SHEET

LEARNING OBJECTIVES

We are coming to the end of the accounting cycle, and certain things must be done at the end of the period that are not done during the regular accounting period. In Chapter 5, adjusting entries and the work sheet are presented.

Objective 1.   Prepare end-of-period adjustments.

In Chapters 2 through 4, we learned how to account for business transactions—events based primarily on arm's length exchanges with other parties. During the accounting period, however, other changes occur which affect the financial condition of the business. For example, supplies are being used, equipment is wearing out, insurance is expiring, and employees may have earned wages that have not yet been paid. It is important for information reported on the financial statements to accurately reflect the results of business transactions with outside parties <u>and</u> other activities taking place inside the business. Therefore, adjustments must be made at the end of the accounting period to properly report assets and liabilities on the balance sheet and to comply with the revenue recognition and matching principles. The **revenue recognition principle** states that revenues should be recognized when earned, regardless of when cash is received from the customer. Revenues are considered earned when a service is provided or a product sold. Similarly, the **expense recognition principle** states that expenses should be recognized when incurred, regardless of when cash is paid. Expenses are generally considered incurred when services are received or assets are consumed. The proper matching of revenues earned during an accounting period with the expenses incurred to produce the revenues is often referred to as the **matching principle**. This approach offers the best measure of net income.

Objective 2.   Post adjusting entries to the general ledger.

After the adjusting entries are journalized, the next step is to post them to the general ledger. The word "Adjusting" is written in the Item column in the general ledger, and each adjustment is posted to the proper general ledger account.

Objective 3.   Prepare a work sheet.

The work sheet is a tool used by accountants to help organize work done at the end of the accounting period. This document is not a formal part of the accounting system. Therefore, information recorded here has no effect on the accounts or financial statements. The main purposes of the work sheet are to prepare the adjusting entries and accumulate information that will be used in the preparation of the financial statements. Five steps are taken to prepare a work sheet.

Step 1	Prepare a trial balance to ensure that the general ledger is in balance before adjusting the accounts.
Step 2	Analyze and enter the adjusting entries in the Adjustments columns of the work sheet. Every adjustment must have an equal debit and credit; and upon completion, the total debits and credits must be equal in the Adjustments columns.
Step 3	Prepare the adjusted trial balance. Every account appearing in the Trial Balance columns will be extended to the Adjusted Trial Balance columns and include any changes due to the adjusting entries. Upon completion, the total of the debits and credits in the Adjusted Trial Balance columns must be equal.
Step 4	Extend the balances in the adjusted trial balance to either the Income Statement or Balance Sheet columns. All revenue and expenses are extended to the Income Statement columns. All other accounts (assets, liabilities, owner's capital, owner's drawing) are extended to the Balance Sheet columns.

Step 5   Complete the work sheet. Initially, the totals of the Income Statement columns will not be equal. Similarly, the totals of the Balance Sheet columns will not be equal. If the Income Statement Credit column exceeds the Income Statement Debit column, the difference represents net income. If the Income Statement Debit column exceeds the Income Statement Credit column, the difference represents net loss. The difference in the Balance Sheet columns will be exactly the same as the difference in the Income Statement columns. The amount of net income should be added to the Income Statement Debit column and the Balance Sheet Credit column for total debits to equal total credits for all four columns. If there is a net loss, this amount should be added to the Income Statement Credit column and the Balance Sheet Debit column.

Partial Work Sheet

| | For Net Income | | | | | For Net Loss | | | |
| | Income Statement | | Balance Sheet | | | Income Statement | | Balance Sheet | |
	Debit	Credit	Debit	Credit		Debit	Credit	Debit	Credit
Net Income	2,500	3,200	6,200	5,500	Net Loss	3,000	2,500	7,000	7,500
	700			700			500	500	
	3,200	3,200	6,200	6,200		3,000	3,000	7,500	7,500

Apart   Together

Objective 4.   Describe methods for finding errors on the work sheet.

The following tips may help in finding errors on the work sheet:

1. Check the addition of all columns.
2. Check the addition and subtraction required when extending to the Adjusted Trial Balance columns.
3. Make sure the adjusted account balances have been extended to the appropriate columns.
4. Make sure that the net income or net loss has been added to the appropriate columns.

Objective 5.   Journalize adjusting entries from the work sheet.

Once the adjustments have been "penciled in" on the work sheet, the next step is to journalize the adjusting entries. "Adjusting Entries" is written in the Description column in the general journal, and the adjusting entries are copied from the work sheet into the general journal.

Objective 6.   Explain the cash, modified cash, and accrual bases of accounting.

The *accrual basis* of accounting recognizes revenues when earned, regardless of when cash is received from the customer. Likewise, expenses are recognized when incurred, regardless of when they are actually paid. The *cash basis* is used by some small businesses and by individuals for income tax purposes. With the cash basis, no revenue or expenses are recognized until cash is actually received or paid.

The *modified cash basis* is a combination of the accrual and cash methods. Revenues and most expenses are recorded only when cash is received or paid (like the cash basis). However, when cash is paid for assets with useful lives greater than one accounting period, exceptions are made. Cash payments like these are recorded as assets, and adjustments are made each period as under the accrual basis. Figure 5-25 in the text compares these methods in different types of transactions.

REVIEW QUESTIONS

Instructions: Analyze each of the following items carefully before writing your answer in the column at the right.

	Question	Answer

LO 1 1. The revenue recognition principle requires revenues to be recognized when _____. .... _____

LO 1 2. The **expense recognition principle** states that expenses should be recognized when... _____

LO 1 3. The matching principle in accounting requires the matching of _____ and _____. .... _____

LO 1 4. The asset account Supplies is adjusted to the income statement account entitled _____. .... _____

LO 1 5. The asset account Prepaid Insurance is adjusted to the income statement account entitled _____. .... _____

LO 1 6. The adjustment to Wages Expense will also affect a liability account called _____. .... _____

LO 1 7. The period of time a plant asset is expected to help produce revenues is called its _____. .... _____

LO 1 8. The purpose of _____ is to spread the cost of a plant asset over its useful life. .... _____

LO 1 9. A plant asset's original cost less salvage value is called _____. _____

LO 1 10. A _____ has a credit balance and is deducted from the related asset account on the balance sheet. .... _____

LO 1 11. The depreciation adjusting entry consists of a debit to Depreciation Expense and a credit to _____. .... _____

LO 1 12. The difference between the original cost of a plant asset and its accumulated depreciation is called _____. .... _____

LO 3 13. A _____ is helpful in preparing end-of-period adjustments and financial statements. .... _____

LO 3 14. The first two monetary columns of a work sheet are called the _____ columns. .... _____

LO 3 15. To which columns of the work sheet are asset and liability accounts extended? .... _____

LO 3 16. To which columns of the work sheet are revenue and expense accounts extended? .... _____

LO 3 17. To which columns of the work sheet are the capital and drawing accounts extended? .... _____

LO 3 18. If the total of the Income Statement Credit column exceeds the total of the Debit column, the business has earned _____. .... _____

LO 6 19. In the _____ basis of accounting, revenues are recorded when earned and expenses are recorded when incurred, regardless of when cash is received or paid. .... _____

LO 6 20. In the _____ basis of accounting, revenues are recorded only when cash is received and expenses are recorded only when cash is paid. .... _____

LO 6 21. The _____ basis of accounting uses the cash basis for revenues and most expenses. .... _____

LO 6 22. Many small professional _____ businesses use the modified cash basis of accounting. .... _____

EXERCISES

Exercise 1 (LO 1) PREPARING END-OF-PERIOD ADJUSTMENTS: SUPPLIES

The beginning balance of the supplies account was $300. During the year, additional supplies costing $600 were purchased and entered as debits to the supplies account. An end-of-period inventory determined that $200 worth of supplies are still on hand.

Required:

1. Determine the balance of the supplies account just prior to making any end-of-period adjustments. _____

2. When preparing the balance sheet, what should be reported for Supplies at the end of the year? _____

3. Determine the balance of the supplies expense account just prior to making any end-of-period adjustments. _____

4. When preparing the income statement, what should be reported for Supplies Expense? (What was the cost of the supplies used?) _____

5. What adjustment must be made to the supplies and supplies expense accounts? _____

Exercise 2 (LO 1) PREPARING END-OF-PERIOD ADJUSTMENTS: DEPRECIATION

Office equipment with an expected life of 10 years and no salvage value was purchased on January 1 for $5,000. Assume the business has no other office equipment and straight-line depreciation is used.

Required:

1. What is the balance of the office equipment account at the end of the year? _____

2. What expense amount should be reported on the income statement for the use of the office equipment? _____

3. What book value should be reported on the balance sheet for the office equipment at the end of the first year? _____

4. What adjustment must be made at the end of the year to report information about the office equipment on the income statement and balance sheet? _____

Exercise 3 (LO 1/2) PREPARING, JOURNALIZING, AND POSTING ADJUSTING ENTRIES: SUPPLIES

The Maddie Hays modeling agency began the current period with office supplies that cost $1,225. During the period, additional supplies costing $4,545 were purchased. At the end of the accounting period, December 31, 20--, only $800 in supplies remain.

Required:

1. Enter the appropriate adjusting entry in a two-column journal.
2. Post this entry to the ledger accounts provided on the next page.

Exercise 3 (Concluded)

1.   **GENERAL JOURNAL**   PAGE 5

	DATE	DESCRIPTION	POST. REF.	DEBIT	CREDIT	
1						1
2						2
3						3
4						4
5						5

2.   **GENERAL LEDGER**

ACCOUNT: Supplies   ACCOUNT NO. 141

DATE		ITEM	POST. REF.	DEBIT	CREDIT	BALANCE DEBIT	BALANCE CREDIT
20--							
Jan.	1	Balance	✔			1 2 2 5 00	
Feb.	12		J2	4 5 4 5 00		5 7 7 0 00	

ACCOUNT: Supplies Expense   ACCOUNT NO. 524

DATE	ITEM	POST. REF.	DEBIT	CREDIT	BALANCE DEBIT	BALANCE CREDIT

Exercise 4 (LO 1/2) PREPARING, JOURNALIZING, AND POSTING ADJUSTING ENTRIES: DEPRECIATION

The Billy Willis Detective Agency began the accounting period by purchasing three cars that cost a total of $75,000. The estimated useful life of these cars is only two years with no salvage value.

Required:

1. Enter the appropriate adjusting entry at the end of the first year in a two-column journal. Willis uses straight-line depreciation.
2. Post this entry to the ledger accounts provided on the next page.

Exercise 4 (Concluded)

1.   **GENERAL JOURNAL**   PAGE   5

	DATE	DESCRIPTION	POST. REF.	DEBIT	CREDIT	
1						1
2						2
3						3
4						4

2.   **GENERAL LEDGER**

ACCOUNT: Automobiles   ACCOUNT NO.   185

DATE		ITEM	POST. REF.	DEBIT	CREDIT	BALANCE DEBIT	BALANCE CREDIT
20--							
Jan.	2		J1	75 0 0 0 00		75 0 0 0 00	

ACCOUNT: Accumulated Depreciation—Automobiles   ACCOUNT NO.   185.1

DATE	ITEM	POST. REF.	DEBIT	CREDIT	BALANCE DEBIT	BALANCE CREDIT

ACCOUNT: Depreciation Expense—Automobiles   ACCOUNT NO.   541

DATE	ITEM	POST. REF.	DEBIT	CREDIT	BALANCE DEBIT	BALANCE CREDIT

Exercise 5 (LO 1/2) PREPARING, JOURNALIZING, AND POSTING ADJUSTING ENTRIES: PREPAID INSURANCE AND WAGES PAYABLE

On June 1, the Straw Basket Herb Farm purchased a one-year liability insurance policy for $600.

As of June 30, an additional $120 was earned by the employees but not yet paid.

Required:

1. Enter the appropriate adjusting entries at the end of June in the following general journal.

2. Post the entries to the ledger accounts provided.

1.   **GENERAL JOURNAL**   PAGE 6

	DATE	DESCRIPTION	POST. REF.	DEBIT	CREDIT	
1						1
2						2
3						3
4						4
5						5
6						6
7						7

2.   **GENERAL LEDGER**

ACCOUNT: Prepaid Insurance   ACCOUNT NO. 145

DATE	ITEM	POST. REF.	DEBIT	CREDIT	BALANCE DEBIT	BALANCE CREDIT
20-- June 1		J2	6 0 0 00		6 0 0 00	

ACCOUNT: Wages Payable   ACCOUNT NO. 219

DATE	ITEM	POST. REF.	DEBIT	CREDIT	BALANCE DEBIT	BALANCE CREDIT

Exercise 5 (Concluded)

ACCOUNT: Wages Expense   ACCOUNT NO. 511

DATE		ITEM	POST. REF.	DEBIT	CREDIT	BALANCE	
						DEBIT	CREDIT
20--							
June	14		J5	5 0 0 00		5 0 0 00	
	28		J5	5 0 0 00		1 0 0 0 00	

ACCOUNT: Insurance Expense   ACCOUNT NO. 535

DATE	ITEM	POST. REF.	DEBIT	CREDIT	BALANCE	
					DEBIT	CREDIT

Exercise 6 (LO 6) CASH BASIS OF ACCOUNTING

In the space provided, indicate which account is debited and which account is credited, using the **cash basis** of accounting. If no entry is made, write "NO ENTRY."

1. Paid rent, $500.

   _____

   _____

2. Purchased typewriter (office equipment) for $300.

   _____

   _____

3. Revenue for week: $300 cash, $200 on account.

   _____

   _____

4. Purchased fax machine (office equipment) for $400, on account.

   _____

   _____

5. Made payment on fax machine, $100.

   _____

   _____

Exercise 7 (LO 6) MODIFIED CASH BASIS OF ACCOUNTING

In the space provided, indicate which account is debited and which account is credited, using the **modified cash basis** of accounting. If no entry is made, write "NO ENTRY."

1. Paid electricity bill, $50.

2. Purchased office equipment for $500, on account.

3. Revenue for week: $500 cash, $200 on account.

4. Wages earned but not paid, $500.

5. Made payment on office equipment previously purchased, $25.

Exercise 8 (LO 6) ACCRUAL BASIS OF ACCOUNTING

In the space provided, indicate which account is debited and which account is credited, using the **accrual basis** of accounting. If no entry is made, write "NO ENTRY."

1. Purchased supplies (prepaid asset), $500, on account.

2. Revenue for week: $400 cash, $250 on account.

3. Wages earned but not paid, $250.

Exercise 8 (Concluded)

4. Made payment on account, $50, for supplies previously purchased.

_____

_____

5. Depreciation on long-term assets, $300.

_____

_____

PROBLEMS

Problem 9 (LO1/3) PREPARING ADJUSTMENTS AND THE WORK SHEET

Kim Ho offers employment counseling to middle managers unemployed due to corporate downsizing. On January 1 of the current year, Ho purchased office equipment with an expected life of 12 years and no salvage value. Computer equipment with an expected life of four years and no salvage value was purchased on July 1 of the current year. Ho uses straight-line depreciation. Office supplies on hand at year-end amounted to $150. Employees earned $300 in wages that have not yet been paid. Provided are the general ledger accounts as of December 31, prior to adjustment.

Required:

1. Using the ledger accounts, complete the Trial Balance columns of the year-end work sheet provided.

2. Prepare the necessary year-end adjustments.

3. Complete the work sheet.

GENERAL LEDGER

ACCOUNT: **Cash**   ACCOUNT NO. 101

DATE		ITEM	POST. REF.	DEBIT	CREDIT	BALANCE DEBIT	BALANCE CREDIT
20--							
Dec.	1	Balance	✔			2 4 0 0 00	
	21		J20	10 8 0 0 00		13 2 0 0 00	
	27		J20		4 2 0 0 00	9 0 0 0 00	

ACCOUNT: **Office Supplies**   ACCOUNT NO. 142

DATE		ITEM	POST. REF.	DEBIT	CREDIT	BALANCE DEBIT	BALANCE CREDIT
20--							
Dec.	1	Balance	✔			2 0 0 00	
	6		J20	3 0 0 00		5 0 0 00	

Problem 9 (Continued)

ACCOUNT: Office Equipment

ACCOUNT NO. 181

DATE		ITEM	POST. REF.	DEBIT	CREDIT	BALANCE	
						DEBIT	CREDIT
20-- Dec.	1	Balance	✔			6 0 0 0 00	

ACCOUNT: Accumulated Depreciation—Office Equipment

ACCOUNT NO. 181.1

DATE	ITEM	POST. REF.	DEBIT	CREDIT	BALANCE	
					DEBIT	CREDIT

ACCOUNT: Computer Equipment

ACCOUNT NO. 187

DATE		ITEM	POST. REF.	DEBIT	CREDIT	BALANCE	
						DEBIT	CREDIT
20-- Dec.	1	Balance	✔			8 0 0 0 00	

ACCOUNT: Accumulated Depreciation—Computer Equipment

ACCOUNT NO. 187.1

DATE	ITEM	POST. REF.	DEBIT	CREDIT	BALANCE	
					DEBIT	CREDIT

ACCOUNT: Accounts Payable

ACCOUNT NO. 202

DATE		ITEM	POST. REF.	DEBIT	CREDIT	BALANCE	
						DEBIT	CREDIT
20-- Dec.	1	Balance	✔				3 0 0 00
	6		J20		2 0 0 00		5 0 0 00
	27		J20	1 0 0 00			4 0 0 00

Problem 9 (Continued)

ACCOUNT: Wages Payable   ACCOUNT NO. 219

DATE	ITEM	POST. REF.	DEBIT	CREDIT	BALANCE DEBIT	BALANCE CREDIT

ACCOUNT: Kim Ho, Capital   ACCOUNT NO. 311

DATE	ITEM	POST. REF.	DEBIT	CREDIT	BALANCE DEBIT	BALANCE CREDIT
20-- Dec. 1	Balance	✔				10 2 0 0 00

ACCOUNT: Kim Ho, Drawing   ACCOUNT NO. 312

DATE	ITEM	POST. REF.	DEBIT	CREDIT	BALANCE DEBIT	BALANCE CREDIT
20-- Dec. 1	Balance	✔			1 5 0 0 00	
30		J20	1 0 0 0 00		2 5 0 0 00	

ACCOUNT: Counseling Fees   ACCOUNT NO. 401

DATE	ITEM	POST. REF.	DEBIT	CREDIT	BALANCE DEBIT	BALANCE CREDIT
20-- Dec. 1	Balance	✔				22 0 0 0 00
31		J20		10 1 7 0 00		32 1 7 0 00

Problem 9 (Continued)

ACCOUNT: Wages Expense   ACCOUNT NO.   511

DATE		ITEM	POST. REF.	DEBIT	CREDIT	BALANCE	
						DEBIT	CREDIT
20-- Dec.	1	Balance	✔			7 0 0 0 00	
	31		J20	1 5 0 0 00		8 5 0 0 00	

ACCOUNT: Rent Expense   ACCOUNT NO.   521

DATE		ITEM	POST. REF.	DEBIT	CREDIT	BALANCE	
						DEBIT	CREDIT
20-- Dec.	1	Balance	✔			4 4 0 0 00	
	4		J20	1 2 0 0 00		5 6 0 0 00	

ACCOUNT: Supplies Expense   ACCOUNT NO.   524

DATE		ITEM	POST. REF.	DEBIT	CREDIT	BALANCE	
						DEBIT	CREDIT

ACCOUNT: Utilities Expense   ACCOUNT NO.   533

DATE		ITEM	POST. REF.	DEBIT	CREDIT	BALANCE	
						DEBIT	CREDIT
20-- Dec.	1	Balance	✔			1 3 0 0 00	
	31		J20	5 7 0 00		1 8 7 0 00	

Problem 9 (Continued)

ACCOUNT: Depreciation Expense—Office Equipment ACCOUNT NO. 541

DATE	ITEM	POST. REF.	DEBIT	CREDIT	BALANCE DEBIT	BALANCE CREDIT

ACCOUNT: Depreciation Expense—Computer Equipment ACCOUNT NO. 542

DATE	ITEM	POST. REF.	DEBIT	CREDIT	BALANCE DEBIT	BALANCE CREDIT

ACCOUNT: Miscellaneous Expense ACCOUNT NO. 549

DATE		ITEM	POST. REF.	DEBIT	CREDIT	BALANCE DEBIT	BALANCE CREDIT
20— Dec.	1	Balance	✔			6 0 0 00	
	22		J20	2 0 0 00		8 0 0 00	

Problem 9 (Continued)

1., 2., and 3.

KIM HO EMPLOYMENT

WORK

FOR YEAR ENDED

	ACCOUNT TITLE	TRIAL BALANCE		ADJUSTMENTS	
		DEBIT	CREDIT	DEBIT	CREDIT
1					
2					
3					
4					
5					
6					
7					
8					
9					
10					
11					
12					
13					
14					
15					
16					
17					
18					
19					
20					
21					
22					
23					
24					
25					
26					
27					
28					
29					
30					
31					

Problem 9 (Concluded)

COUNSELING SERVICES

SHEET

DECEMBER 31, 20--

ADJUSTED TRIAL BALANCE		INCOME STATEMENT		BALANCE SHEET		
DEBIT	CREDIT	DEBIT	CREDIT	DEBIT	CREDIT	
						1
						2
						3
						4
						5
						6
						7
						8
						9
						10
						11
						12
						13
						14
						15
						16
						17
						18
						19
						20
						21
						22
						23
						24
						25
						26
						27
						28
						29
						30
						31

Problem 10 (LO 1/3) PREPARING ADJUSTMENTS AND THE WORK SHEET

The trial balance for Juan's Speedy Delivery Service as of September 30, 20--, is shown on the work sheet that follows.

Data to complete the adjustments are as follows:

(a) Supplies inventory as of September 30, $450.
(b) Insurance expired, $200.
(c) Depreciation on delivery equipment, $350.
(d) Wages earned by employees but not paid as of September 30, $215.

Required:

1. Enter the adjustments in the Adjustments columns on the work sheet.
2. Complete the work sheet.

1. and 2.

JUAN'S SPEEDY

WORK

FOR MONTH ENDED

	ACCOUNT TITLE	TRIAL BALANCE DEBIT	TRIAL BALANCE CREDIT	ADJUSTMENTS DEBIT	ADJUSTMENTS CREDIT
1	Cash	1 5 4 5 00			
2	Accounts Receivable	8 5 0 00			
3	Supplies	7 2 5 00			
4	Prepaid Insurance	1 5 0 0 00			
5	Delivery Equipment	6 3 0 0 00			
6	Accum. Depr.—Delivery Equip.				
7	Accounts Payable		9 8 0 00		
8	Wages Payable				
9	Juan Garcia, Capital		9 0 0 0 00		
10	Juan Garcia, Drawing	1 2 0 0 00			
11	Delivery Fees		5 2 4 0 00		
12	Wages Expense	1 4 7 5 00			
13	Advertising Expense	4 2 0 00			
14	Rent Expense	7 5 0 00			
15	Supplies Expense				
16	Phone Expense	1 8 0 00			
17	Insurance Expense				
18	Repair Expense	1 9 0 00			
19	Oil and Gas Expense	8 5 00			
20	Depreciation Expense—Del. Equip.				
21		15 2 2 0 00	15 2 2 0 00		
22					
23					

Problem 10 (Concluded)

DELIVERY SERVICE

SHEET

SEPTEMBER 30, 20--

ADJUSTED TRIAL BALANCE		INCOME STATEMENT		BALANCE SHEET		
DEBIT	CREDIT	DEBIT	CREDIT	DEBIT	CREDIT	
						1
						2
						3
						4
						5
						6
						7
						8
						9
						10
						11
						12
						13
						14
						15
						16
						17
						18
						19
						20
						21
						22
						23

Problem 11 (LO 4) FINDING AND CORRECTING ERRORS ON A WORK SHEET

A work sheet for George Green's Landscaping Service follows. It should include these adjustments.

(a)   Ending inventory of supplies as of July 31, $350.
(b)   Insurance expired as of July 31, $225.
(c)   Depreciation on tractor, $460.
(d)   Wages earned but not paid as of July 31, $320.

Required:

Errors have been intentionally placed in this work sheet. Review the work sheet for addition mistakes, transpositions, and other errors and make all necessary corrections.

(*Note:* Errors are intentional.)

GREEN'S LANDSCAPING

WORK

FOR MONTH ENDED

	ACCOUNT TITLE	TRIAL BALANCE DEBIT	TRIAL BALANCE CREDIT	ADJUSTMENTS DEBIT	ADJUSTMENTS CREDIT
1	Cash	1 8 2 5 00			
2	Accounts Receivable	7 2 0 00			
3	Supplies	6 0 0 00			(a) 3 5 0 00
4	Prepaid Insurance	8 5 0 00			(b) 2 2 5 00
5	Tractor	6 5 5 0 00			(c) 4 6 0 00
6	Accum. Depr.—Tractor				
7	Accounts Payable		5 2 0 00		
8	Wages Payable				(d) 3 2 0 00
9	George Green, Capital		8 2 5 0 00		
10	George Green, Drawing	1 2 0 0 00			
11	Landscaping Fees		6 1 0 0 00		
12	Wages Expense	1 5 4 0 00		(d) 3 2 0 00	
13	Advertising Expense	2 5 0 00			
14	Rent Expense	7 7 5 00			
15	Supplies Expense			(a) 3 5 0 00	
16	Phone Expense	1 4 0 00			
17	Utilities Expense	2 2 0 00			
18	Insurance Expense			(b) 2 2 5 00	
19	Depr. Expense—Tractor			(c) 4 6 0 00	
20	Miscellaneous Expense	2 0 0 00			
21		14 8 7 0 00	14 8 7 0 00	1 3 5 5 00	1 3 5 5 00
22	Net Income				
23					

Problem 11 (Concluded)

SERVICE

SHEET

JULY 31, 20--

ADJUSTED TRIAL BALANCE		INCOME STATEMENT		BALANCE SHEET		
DEBIT	CREDIT	DEBIT	CREDIT	DEBIT	CREDIT	
1 8 2 5 00				1 8 2 5 00		1
7 2 0 00				7 2 0 00		2
2 5 0 00				2 5 0 00		3
6 5 0 00				6 5 0 00		4
6 0 9 0 00				6 0 9 0 00		5
						6
	5 2 0 00				5 2 0 00	7
	3 2 0 00		3 2 0 00			8
	8 2 5 0 00				8 2 5 0 00	9
1 2 0 0 00		1 2 0 0 00				10
	6 1 0 0 00		6 1 0 0 00			11
1 5 4 0 00		1 5 4 0 00			1 8 4 0 00	12
2 5 0 00		2 5 0 00				13
7 7 5 00		7 7 5 00				14
3 5 0 00		3 5 0 00				15
1 4 0 00		1 4 0 00				16
2 2 0 00		2 2 0 00				17
2 2 5 00		2 2 5 00				18
4 6 0 00		4 6 0 00				19
2 0 0 00		2 0 0 00				20
13 3 5 5 00	15 1 9 0 00	2 4 1 7 00	6 4 2 0 00	8 3 4 7 00	8 7 7 0 00	21
		1 7 2 0 00			1 7 2 0 00	22
		4 1 3 7 00	6 4 2 0 00	8 3 4 7 00	10 4 9 0 00	23

Problem 12 (LO 6) CASH, MODIFIED CASH, AND ACCRUAL BASES

Mark Mosley has his own consulting business. Listed below are selected transactions from the month of April.

Apr.	1	Paid office rent, $500.
	2	Purchased office supplies, $250.
	3	Purchased office equipment on account, $1,000.
	4	Earned consulting fees: $400 cash, $150 on account.
	5	Paid phone bill, $48.
	6	Purchased one-year insurance policy, $200.
	7	Paid $100 on account (for office equipment previously purchased).
	8	Received $150 on account from a customer (previously owed).
	9	Recorded depreciation on office equipment for month, $50.

Required:

Record the transactions in the space provided, using the following bases:

1. The cash basis.

2. The modified cash basis.

3. The accrual basis.

Problem 12 (Continued)

1. Cash Basis

GENERAL JOURNAL   PAGE

	DATE	DESCRIPTION	POST. REF.	DEBIT	CREDIT	
1						1
2						2
3						3
4						4
5						5
6						6
7						7
8						8
9						9
10						10
11						11
12						12
13						13
14						14
15						15
16						16
17						17
18						18
19						19
20						20
21						21
22						22
23						23
24						24
25						25
26						26
27						27
28						28
29						29
30						30

Problem 12 (Continued)

2. Modified Cash Basis

GENERAL JOURNAL   PAGE

	DATE		DESCRIPTION	POST. REF.	DEBIT	CREDIT	
1							1
2							2
3							3
4							4
5							5
6							6
7							7
8							8
9							9
10							10
11							11
12							12
13							13
14							14
15							15
16							16
17							17
18							18
19							19
20							20
21							21
22							22
23							23
24							24
25							25
26							26
27							27
28							28
29							29
30							30

Problem 12 (Concluded)

3. Accrual Basis

GENERAL JOURNAL   PAGE

	DATE		DESCRIPTION	POST. REF.	DEBIT	CREDIT	
1							1
2							2
3							3
4							4
5							5
6							6
7							7
8							8
9							9
10							10
11							11
12							12
13							13
14							14
15							15
16							16
17							17
18							18
19							19
20							20
21							21
22							22
23							23
24							24
25							25
26							26
27							27
28							28
29							29
30							30

CHAPTER 5 APPENDIX
DEPRECIATION METHODS

APPENDIX LEARNING OBJECTIVES

In Chapter 5, the straight-line method of depreciation was illustrated. In the appendix to Chapter 5, three additional methods are explained. These methods are used when a different schedule of expenses provides a more appropriate matching with the revenues generated.

Objective 1. **Prepare a depreciation schedule using the straight-line method.**
Objective 2. **Prepare a depreciation schedule using the sum-of-the-years'-digits method.**
Objective 3. **Prepare a depreciation schedule using the double-declining-balance method.**
Objective 4. **Prepare a depreciation schedule for tax purposes using the Modified Accelerated Cost Recovery System.**

Apx. Exercise 1 (LO 1) STRAIGHT-LINE DEPRECIATION

Office equipment was purchased on January 1 at a cost of $48,000. It has an estimated useful life of four years and a salvage value of $6,000. Prepare a depreciation schedule showing the depreciation expense, accumulated depreciation, and book value for each year under the straight-line method.

STRAIGHT-LINE DEPRECIATION

Apx. Exercise 2 (LO 2) SUM-OF-THE-YEARS'-DIGITS DEPRECIATION

Using the information given in Exercise 1, prepare a depreciation schedule showing the depreciation expense, accumulated depreciation, and book value for each year under the sum-of-the-years'-digits method.

SUM-OF-THE-YEARS'-DIGITS DEPRECIATION

Apx. Exercise 3 (LO 3) DOUBLE-DECLINING-BALANCE DEPRECIATION

Using the information given in Exercise 1, prepare a depreciation schedule showing the depreciation expense, accumulated depreciation, and book value for each year under the double-declining-balance method.

DOUBLE-DECLINING-BALANCE DEPRECIATION

Apx. Exercise 4 (LO 4) DEPRECIATION UNDER THE MODIFIED ACCELERATED COST RECOVERY SYSTEM

Using the information given in Exercise 1 and the rates shown in Figure 5A-4 of the text, prepare a depreciation schedule showing the depreciation expense, accumulated depreciation, and book value for each year under the Modified Accelerated Cost Recovery System. For tax purposes, assume that the office equipment has a useful life of five years. (The IRS schedule will spread depreciation over six years.) Round to the nearest dollar.

MODIFIED ACCELERATED COST RECOVERY SYSTEM

CHAPTER 6
FINANCIAL STATEMENTS AND THE CLOSING PROCESS

LEARNING OBJECTIVES

Chapter 5 introduced the work sheet and demonstrated how it is used to prepare year-end adjustments. Chapter 6 completes the discussion of the work sheet by illustrating its role in the preparation of financial statements and closing entries. The purpose of the post-closing trial balance is also explained. It is prepared after closing entries have been posted to the general ledger accounts.

Objective 1.   Prepare financial statements with the aid of a work sheet.

The work sheet contains almost all the information needed to prepare the income statement, the statement of owner's equity, and the balance sheet. Numbers can be taken directly from the Income Statement columns for the income statement. The owner's capital account must be reviewed before completing the statement of owner's equity. If additional investments were made, they must be added to the beginning capital balance to compute the total investment. The net income (or net loss) is added to the total investment, and withdrawals (drawing) are subtracted, giving the ending owner's equity. The balance sheet is prepared using the ending owner's equity balance reported on the statement of owner's equity and the permanent accounts listed in the Balance Sheet columns of the work sheet.

Objective 2.   Journalize and post closing entries.

After the work sheet is completed, the financial statements are prepared. Then the adjusting and closing entries are journalized and posted. All temporary accounts need zero balances to begin the new accounting period. The closing process has four journal entries:

1.   to close revenue account(s) to Income Summary,
2.   to close expense accounts to Income Summary,
3.   to close Income Summary to the owner's capital account, and
4.   to close Drawing to the owner's capital account.

Objective 3.   Prepare a post-closing trial balance.

The **post-closing trial balance** lists all the permanent accounts that have balances to begin the new accounting period. It is prepared to prove the equality of the debit and credit balances in the general ledger accounts following the closing process. Since temporary accounts (drawing, revenues, and expenses) are closed at the end of the period, they do not appear on the post-closing trial balance.

Objective 4.   List and describe the steps in the accounting cycle.

This chapter concludes the accounting cycle that began in Chapter 1. The 10 steps are as follows:

During the Accounting Period
1.   Analyze source documents.
2.   Journalize the transactions.
3.   Post to the general ledger accounts.

End of Accounting Period
4.   Prepare a trial balance.
5.   Determine and prepare the needed adjustments on the work sheet.

6. Complete an end-of-period work sheet.
7. Journalize and post the adjusting entries.
8. Prepare an income statement, a statement of owner's equity, and a balance sheet.
9. Journalize and post the closing entries.
10. Prepare a post-closing trial balance.

REVIEW QUESTIONS

Instructions: Analyze each of the following items carefully before writing your answer in the column at the right.

	Question	**Answer**
LO 1 1.	The work sheet provides most of the needed information to prepare which three financial statements?	_____
LO 1 2.	The income statement contains which two major types of accounts?	_____
LO 1 3.	The statement of owner's equity adds _____ to the owner's investment and subtracts _____.	_____ _____
LO 1 4.	Amounts owed that will be paid within a year are called _____.	_____
LO 1 5.	Expenses are listed on the income statement in the order they appear on the chart of accounts or in descending order by _____ amount.	_____
LO 1 6.	To find if the owner made any additional investments during the period, we must review the _____ account in the general ledger.	_____
LO 1 7.	When net income and additional investments are greater than withdrawals, the difference is called a(n) _____ in capital for the month.	_____
LO 1 8.	When the balance sheet is shown in _____ form, liabilities and owner's equity sections are placed below the assets section.	_____
LO 1 9.	When the balance sheet is shown in _____ form, assets are on the left and liabilities and owner's equity are on the right.	_____
LO 1 10.	A(n) _____ balance sheet groups similar items together such as current assets and current liabilities.	_____
LO 1 11.	Cash and assets that will be converted to cash or consumed within a year or the normal operating cycle are called _____ assets. ...	_____
LO 1 12.	The _____ is the period of time required to purchase supplies and services and convert them back into cash.	_____
LO 1 13.	Accounts Payable and Wages Payable are classified as _____ liabilities.	_____
LO 2 14.	Assets, liabilities, and the owner's capital account accumulate information across accounting periods; they are called _____ accounts.	_____

LO 2 15. Revenue, expense, and drawing accounts accumulate information for the specific period only, then they go back to _____ balances.

_____

LO 2 16. Because revenue, expense, and drawing accounts are closed each accounting period, they are called _____ accounts. ....

_____

LO 2 17. The _____ account is used to summarize the effects of revenue and expense accounts; it is then closed to the capital account. ....

_____

LO 2 18. When closing entries are posted to the general ledger, the word _____ is written in the Item column of each general ledger account affected. ....

_____

LO 3 19. The _____ trial balance only lists permanent accounts. ....

_____

LO 4 20. The _____ begins with analyzing source documents and ends with the post-closing trial balance. ....

_____

EXERCISES

Exercise 1 (LO 1) REVIEW: COMPUTE NET INCOME

From the information given below, compute net income.

_____

Revenue:	Delivery Fees	$4,826
Expenses:	Wages Expense	2,700
	Rent Expense	350
	Supplies Expense	55
	Insurance Expense	33
	Depreciation Expense	100

Exercise 2 (LO 1) REVIEW: COMPUTE OWNER'S EQUITY

Using the net income from Exercise 1 and the following information, compute the (a) increase to owner's equity and (b) ending owner's equity balance. Assume no additional investments were made by the owner.

(a) _____

(b) _____

Beginning owner's equity: $5,680
Withdrawals by owner: 1,000

Exercise 3 (LO 2) THE CLOSING PROCESS

Based upon Exercises 1 and 2 above, list the accounts that must be closed at the end of the accounting cycle (in addition to the income summary account).

_____

_____

_____

_____

_____

_____

_____

PROBLEMS

Problems 4–9

To complete Problems 4 through 9, use the completed work sheet for Collins Cycle Service as of April 30, 20--, below and the general ledger on pages 88-92.

COLLINS CYCLE

WORK

FOR MONTH ENDED

	ACCOUNT TITLE	TRIAL BALANCE DEBIT	TRIAL BALANCE CREDIT	ADJUSTMENTS DEBIT	ADJUSTMENTS CREDIT
1	Cash	4 8 0 0 00			
2	Supplies	8 2 6 00			(a) 3 2 6 00
3	Prepaid Insurance	1 3 0 0 00			(b) 2 0 0 00
4	Repair Equipment	2 6 0 0 00			
5	Accum. Depr.—Repair Equip.		4 0 0 00		(c) 4 0 0 00
6	Accounts Payable		1 3 0 0 00		
7	Wages Payable				(d) 1 0 0 00
8	Jean Collins, Capital		6 0 0 0 00		
9	Jean Collins, Drawing	3 0 0 00			
10	Repair Fees		2 8 3 9 00		
11	Wages Expense	2 7 5 00		(d) 1 0 0 00	
12	Rent Expense	4 0 0 00			
13	Supplies Expense			(a) 3 2 6 00	
14	Phone Expense	3 8 00			
15	Insurance Expense			(b) 2 0 0 00	
16	Depreciation Exp.—Repair Equip.			(c) 4 0 0 00	
17		10 5 3 9 00	10 5 3 9 00	1 0 2 6 00	1 0 2 6 00
18					
19					

Problems 4–9 (Concluded)

SERVICE

SHEET

APRIL 30, 20--

	ADJUSTED TRIAL BALANCE		INCOME STATEMENT		BALANCE SHEET		
	DEBIT	CREDIT	DEBIT	CREDIT	DEBIT	CREDIT	
1	4 8 0 0 00				4 8 0 0 00		1
2	5 0 0 00				5 0 0 00		2
3	1 1 0 0 00				1 1 0 0 00		3
4	2 6 0 0 00				2 6 0 0 00		4
5		8 0 0 00				8 0 0 00	5
6		1 3 0 0 00				1 3 0 0 00	6
7		1 0 0 00				1 0 0 00	7
8		6 0 0 0 00				6 0 0 0 00	8
9	3 0 0 00				3 0 0 00		9
10		2 8 3 9 00		2 8 3 9 00			10
11	3 7 5 00		3 7 5 00				11
12	4 0 0 00		4 0 0 00				12
13	3 2 6 00		3 2 6 00				13
14	3 8 00		3 8 00				14
15	2 0 0 00		2 0 0 00				15
16	4 0 0 00		4 0 0 00				16
17	11 0 3 9 00	11 0 3 9 00	1 7 3 9 00	2 8 3 9 00	9 3 0 0 00	8 2 0 0 00	17
18			1 1 0 0 00			1 1 0 0 00	18
19			2 8 3 9 00	2 8 3 9 00	9 3 0 0 00	9 3 0 0 00	19

Problem 4 REVIEW: PREPARE ADJUSTING ENTRIES

Journalize the adjusting entries and post them to the general ledger accounts. The balances shown in the general ledger accounts are *trial balance* amounts—that is, before adjusting and closing entries are entered.

GENERAL JOURNAL   PAGE 2

	DATE	DESCRIPTION	POST. REF.	DEBIT	CREDIT	
1						1
2						2
3						3
4						4
5						5
6						6
7						7
8						8
9						9
10						10
11						11
12						12
13						13

Use these ledger accounts for Problems 4 and 8.

GENERAL LEDGER

ACCOUNT   Cash   ACCOUNT NO.   101

DATE	ITEM	POST. REF.	DEBIT	CREDIT	BALANCE DEBIT	BALANCE CREDIT
20-- Apr. 30	Balance	✓			4 8 0 0 00	

ACCOUNT   Supplies   ACCOUNT NO.   141

DATE	ITEM	POST. REF.	DEBIT	CREDIT	BALANCE DEBIT	BALANCE CREDIT
20-- Apr. 30	Balance	✓			8 2 6 00	

Problems 4 and 8 (Continued)

ACCOUNT   Prepaid Insurance

ACCOUNT NO.   145

DATE		ITEM	POST. REF.	DEBIT	CREDIT	BALANCE	
						DEBIT	CREDIT
20-- Apr.	30	Balance	✓			1 3 0 0 00	

ACCOUNT   Repair Equipment

ACCOUNT NO.   188

DATE		ITEM	POST. REF.	DEBIT	CREDIT	BALANCE	
						DEBIT	CREDIT
20-- Apr.	30	Balance	✓			2 6 0 0 00	

ACCOUNT   Accumulated Depreciation—Repair Equipment

ACCOUNT NO.   188.1

DATE		ITEM	POST. REF.	DEBIT	CREDIT	BALANCE	
						DEBIT	CREDIT
20-- Apr.	1	Balance	✓				4 0 0 00

ACCOUNT   Accounts Payable

ACCOUNT NO.   202

DATE		ITEM	POST. REF.	DEBIT	CREDIT	BALANCE	
						DEBIT	CREDIT
20-- Apr.	30	Balance	✓				1 3 0 0 00

Problems 4 and 8 (Continued)

ACCOUNT   Wages Payable   ACCOUNT NO.   219

DATE	ITEM	POST. REF.	DEBIT	CREDIT	BALANCE DEBIT	BALANCE CREDIT

ACCOUNT   Jean Collins, Capital   ACCOUNT NO.   311

DATE		ITEM	POST. REF.	DEBIT	CREDIT	BALANCE DEBIT	BALANCE CREDIT
20-- Apr.	1	Balance	✓				5 0 0 0 00
	15		J1		1 0 0 0 00		6 0 0 0 00

ACCOUNT   Jean Collins, Drawing   ACCOUNT NO.   312

DATE		ITEM	POST. REF.	DEBIT	CREDIT	BALANCE DEBIT	BALANCE CREDIT
20-- Apr.	30	Balance	✓			3 0 0 00	

ACCOUNT   Income Summary   ACCOUNT NO.   313

DATE	ITEM	POST. REF.	DEBIT	CREDIT	BALANCE DEBIT	BALANCE CREDIT

Problems 4 and 8 (Continued)

ACCOUNT   Repair Fees   ACCOUNT NO.   401

DATE		ITEM	POST. REF.	DEBIT	CREDIT	BALANCE	
						DEBIT	CREDIT
20-- Apr.	30	Balance	✓				2 8 3 9 00

ACCOUNT   Wages Expense   ACCOUNT NO.   511

DATE		ITEM	POST. REF.	DEBIT	CREDIT	BALANCE	
						DEBIT	CREDIT
20-- Apr.	30	Balance	✓			2 7 5 00	

ACCOUNT   Rent Expense   ACCOUNT NO.   521

DATE		ITEM	POST. REF.	DEBIT	CREDIT	BALANCE	
						DEBIT	CREDIT
20-- Apr.	30	Balance	✓			4 0 0 00	

ACCOUNT   Supplies Expense   ACCOUNT NO.   524

DATE		ITEM	POST. REF.	DEBIT	CREDIT	BALANCE	
						DEBIT	CREDIT

Problems 4 and 8 (Continued)

ACCOUNT   Phone Expense   ACCOUNT NO.   525

DATE		ITEM	POST. REF.	DEBIT	CREDIT	BALANCE	
						DEBIT	CREDIT
20--							
Apr.	30	Balance	✓			3 8 00	

ACCOUNT   Insurance Expense   ACCOUNT NO.   535

DATE		ITEM	POST. REF.	DEBIT	CREDIT	BALANCE	
						DEBIT	CREDIT

ACCOUNT   Depreciation Expense—Repair Equipment   ACCOUNT NO.   542

DATE		ITEM	POST. REF.	DEBIT	CREDIT	BALANCE	
						DEBIT	CREDIT

Problem 5 (LO 1) PREPARE AN INCOME STATEMENT

Prepare the income statement.

Problem 6 (LO 2) PREPARE A STATEMENT OF OWNER'S EQUITY

Prepare the statement of owner's equity. Be sure to check the capital account in the general ledger.

Problem 7 (LO 1) PREPARE A BALANCE SHEET

Prepare the balance sheet in report form.

Problem 8 (LO 2) JOURNALIZING AND POSTING CLOSING ENTRIES

Journalize the closing entries and post them to the general ledger accounts. (The general ledger accounts can be found on pages 88-92.)

GENERAL JOURNAL   PAGE 2

	DATE	DESCRIPTION	POST. REF.	DEBIT	CREDIT	
14						14
15						15
16						16
17						17
18						18
19						19
20						20
21						21
22						22
23						23
24						24
25						25
26						26
27						27
28						28
29						29
30						30
31						31
32						32

Problem 9 (LO 3) PREPARE A POST-CLOSING TRIAL BALANCE

Prepare the post-closing trial balance.

ACCOUNT TITLE	ACCT. NO.	DEBIT BALANCE	CREDIT BALANCE

CHAPTER 6 APPENDIX
STATEMENT OF CASH FLOWS

APPENDIX LEARNING OBJECTIVES

In Chapter 6, we reviewed in greater detail the preparation of three financial statements: the income statement, statement of owner's equity, and balance sheet. A fourth important financial statement is the statement of cash flows. The main purpose of this statement is to report the sources and uses of cash. These sources and uses are categorized into three types of business activities: operating, investing, and financing.

Objective 1.   Classify business transactions as operating, investing, or financing.

Operating activities include those cash flows that are related to the revenues and expenses reported on the income statement. Examples include cash received for services performed and the payment of cash for expenses.

Investing activities are those transactions associated with buying and selling long-term assets, lending money, and collecting the principal on the related loans.

Financing activities are those cash transactions with owners and creditors. Examples include cash received from the owner to finance the operations and cash paid to the owner as withdrawals. Financing activities also include the receipt of cash from loans and the repayment of the loans.

Objective 2.   Prepare a statement of cash flows by analyzing and categorizing a series of business transactions.

The main body of the statement of cash flows consists of three sections: operating, investing, and financing activities.

Name of Business		
Statement of Cash Flows		
For Period Ended Date		

Cash flows from operating activities:		
Cash received from customers		$ x,xxx.xx
List cash paid for various expenses	$ (xxx.xx)	
Total cash paid for operations		(x,xxx.xx)
Net cash provided by (used for) operating activities		$ xxx.xx
Cash flows from investing activities:		
List cash received from the sale of long-term assets and other		
investing activities	$ x,xxx.xx	
List cash paid for the purchase of long-term assets and other		
investing activities	(x,xxx.xx)	
Net cash provided by (used for) investing activities		x,xxx.xx
Cash flows from financing activities:		
List cash received from owners and creditors	$ x,xxx.xx	
List cash paid to owners and creditors	(xxx.xx)	
Net cash provided by (used for) financing activities		x,xxx.xx
Net increase (decrease) in cash		$ xxx.xx

Apx. Exercise 1 REVIEW: ENTERING TRANSACTIONS IN T ACCOUNTS

Sung Joon Lee opened an overseas mailing business, "Lee's Quick Sail." The following transactions occurred during August of the current year. Enter the transactions in the cash T account provided on the next page, identifying each with its corresponding letter.

(a) Lee invested $5,000 in the business.
(b) Paid office rent, $500.
(c) Bought supplies for the month, $200.
(d) Lee made an additional investment in the business, $1,000.
(e) Bought a new scale for $1,200: $700 cash and $500 on account.
(f) Received $600 for mailing services.
(g) Paid $200 on loan [see transaction (e)].
(h) Paid electricity bill, $64.
(i) Paid gas bill, $70.
(j) Received $900 for mailing services.
(k) Paid part-time employee, $90.
(l) Lee withdrew cash for personal use, $400.

Apx. Exercise 1 (Concluded)

CASH

Apx. Exercise 2 REVIEW: FOOTING AND BALANCING A T ACCOUNT

Foot and balance the T account in Exercise 1. The cash balance at the end of August is _____ .

Apx. Problem 3 (LO 1) CLASSIFYING BUSINESS TRANSACTIONS AS OPERATING, INVESTING, OR FINANCING

Label each transaction in the cash T account of Exercise 1 as an operating (O), an investing (I), or a financing (F) activity.

Apx. Problem 4 (LO 2)   PREPARING A STATEMENT OF CASH FLOWS BY ANALYZING BUSINESS TRANSACTIONS

Prepare a statement of cash flows based on the transactions and cash T account in Exercises 1 and 2, and Problem 3.

CHAPTER 7
ACCOUNTING FOR CASH

LEARNING OBJECTIVES

Managing cash is an essential part of every business's operations. In Chapter 7, we explore the cash account—setting up a bank account, writing checks and making deposits, preparing a bank reconciliation and the journal entries needed, operating a petty cash fund, establishing a change fund and using a cash short and over account.

Objective 1.   Describe how to open and use a checking account.

Most banks have standard procedures for opening and using a **checking account.** They begin with a signature card, whereby the depositor's Social Security number or EIN number and signature are provided. Preparing deposit tickets, endorsing properly, and writing checks are parts of using a checking account wisely.

Objective 2.   Prepare a bank reconciliation and related journal entries.

On a monthly basis, banks send **bank statements** to their checking account customers. The bank statement must be reconciled—compared to the checkbook. Adjustments are made to the ending bank balance and the checkbook balance until they are equal. Once the bank reconciliation is prepared, any changes to the book (checkbook) balance will require journal entries.

Objective 3.   Establish and use a petty cash fund.

A **petty cash fund** is both convenient and cost effective. Rather than writing checks for small amounts, costing time and money, a sum of money is set aside for petty (small) cash payments during the month. Vouchers are issued for all money paid out; the petty cash fund is replenished at the end of the month (brought back up to its original amount). A journal entry is made to record all of the expenses shown in the petty cash record.

Objective 4.   Establish a change fund and use the cash short and over account.

Businesses that receive cash from customers generally need to establish a change fund of currency and coins to use in handling cash sales. When many cash transactions occur, there often will be a difference between what the cash register tape says and the amount of cash actually found in the drawer. An account called Cash Short and Over is used to account for these differences. At the end of the month, if there is more cash short than over, it is an expense to the business. If there is more cash over than short, it is a revenue to the business.

REVIEW QUESTIONS

Instructions: Analyze each of the following items carefully before writing your answer in the column at the right.

	Question	**Answer**

LO 1 1. To open a checking account, each person authorized to sign checks must fill out a(n) _____. .... _____

LO 1 2. A(n) _____ lists items being deposited to a checking account. _____

LO 1 3. Each check deposited is identified by its _____. .... _____

LO 1 4. A(n) _____ consists of stamping or writing the depositor's name and other information on the back of a check. .... _____

LO 1 5. A(n) _____ endorsement consists of a signature on the back of a check. .... _____

LO 1 6. A(n) _____ endorsement consists of a signature together with words such as "For Deposit." .... _____

LO 1 7. Depositors using ATMs must first key in their _____. _____

LO 1 8. A(n) _____ is a document ordering a bank to pay cash from the depositor's account. .... _____

LO 1 9. The _____ is the bank on which a check is drawn. .... _____

LO 1 10. The _____ is the person being paid the cash. .... _____

LO 1 11. The _____ is the depositor who orders the bank to pay the cash. _____

LO 1 12. Space is contained to record all relevant information about a check on its _____. .... _____

LO 1 13. A statement issued to the depositor once a month is called a _____. .... _____

LO 1 14. Checks paid by the bank and returned to the depositor are called _____. .... _____

LO 2 15. The process of bringing the bank and book balances into agreement is called preparing a(n) _____. .... _____

LO 2 16. Checks issued during the period but not yet processed by the bank are called _____. .... _____

LO 2 17. Deposits made but not yet recorded by the bank are called _____. _____

LO 2 18. Bank charges for services are called _____. .... _____

LO 2 19. Checks deposited but not paid because the drawer did not have enough money in the account are called _____ checks. .... _____

LO 2 20. Transactions can be completed by _____ rather than by the manual process of writing checks or using cash.............................. _____

LO 3 21. A fund called the _____ is established to pay for small items with cash. .... _____

LO 3   22. A receipt called a(n) _____ is prepared for every payment from the petty cash fund. ....   _____

LO 3   23. The _____ is a special multi-column record where petty cash payments are recorded. ....   _____

LO 3   24. At the end of the month, the petty cash fund is _____, or brought up to its original amount. ....   _____

LO 4   25. The cash short and over account is used when actual cash on hand is different from what is on the _____ tape plus the change fund.   _____

LO 4   26. When actual cash on hand exceeds what is on the register tape plus the change fund, this difference is a(n) _____. ....   _____

LO 4   27. When actual cash on hand is less than what is on the register tape plus the change fund, this difference is a(n) _____. ....   _____

EXERCISES

Exercise 1 (LO1) PREPARE DEPOSIT TICKET

Using the deposit ticket shown below, enter the following information:

Date:	March 28, 20--	Checks:	33-11	$202
Currency:	$318		123-666	48
Coin:	33		2-9	211

Exercise 2 (LO1) PREPARE CHECK AND STUB

During the month of October, you made the following payments by check. Fill in the stubs and write the checks. Use the blank checks provided on page 104. Enter $825.50 as the balance brought forward on Check No. 138, and add a deposit for $85 on October 10.

Oct.   3   Issued Check No. 138 to Emerald Lawn Care, Inc., for work done on the shrubbery around the office building, $125. (Miscellaneous Expense)

8   Issued Check No. 139 to Maxwell Office Supply for stationery, $85.90. (Office Supplies)

10   Issued Check No. 140 to Wesley's Towing for cost of towing company car to repair shop, $50. (Automobile Expense)

Exercise 2 (Concluded)

No. **138**

DATE _____ 20 _____
TO _____
FOR _____
_____
ACCT. _____

	DOLLARS	CENTS
BAL BRO'T FOR'D		
AMT. DEPOSITED		
TOTAL		
AMT. THIS CHECK		
BAL CAR'D FOR'D		

No. **138**   60-55 / 313

_____ 20 _____

PAY
TO THE
ORDER OF _____ $ _____

_____ Dollars

PEOPLE'S BANK   FOR CLASSROOM USE ONLY
Wilkes-Barre, PA 18704-1456

MEMO _____   BY _____

⑆1300555 16 3247 5⑈

No. **139**

DATE _____ 20 _____
TO _____
FOR _____
_____
ACCT. _____

	DOLLARS	CENTS
BAL BRO'T FOR'D		
AMT. DEPOSITED		
TOTAL		
AMT. THIS CHECK		
BAL CAR'D FOR'D		

No. **139**   60-55 / 313

_____ 20 _____

PAY
TO THE
ORDER OF _____ $ _____

_____ Dollars

PEOPLE'S BANK   FOR CLASSROOM USE ONLY
Wilkes-Barre, PA 18704-1456

MEMO _____   BY _____

⑆1300555 16 3247 5⑈

No. **140**

DATE _____ 20 _____
TO _____
FOR _____
_____
ACCT. _____

	DOLLARS	CENTS
BAL BRO'T FOR'D		
AMT. DEPOSITED		
TOTAL		
AMT. THIS CHECK		
BAL CAR'D FOR'D		

No. **140**   60-55 / 313

_____ 20 _____

PAY
TO THE
ORDER OF _____ $ _____

_____ Dollars

PEOPLE'S BANK   FOR CLASSROOM USE ONLY
Wilkes-Barre, PA 18704-1456

MEMO _____   BY _____

⑆1300555 16 3247 5⑈

Exercise 3 (LO2) BANK RECONCILIATION PROCEDURES

The bank reconciliation is a process of matching the checkbook balance with the bank statement balance—adding and subtracting items until the two are equal. In the exercise below, indicate which action is taken.

        a.   Add to checkbook balance.

        b.   Subtract from checkbook balance.

        c.   Add to bank statement balance.

        d.   Subtract from bank statement balance.

_____ 1. Deposits in transit

_____ 2. Error in checkbook whereby a check for $128 was entered into the checkbook as $182

_____ 3. NSF check

_____ 4. Checks outstanding (not yet processed by the bank)

_____ 5. Bank service fees

_____ 6. Credit memo, telling depositor that a note was collected

_____ 7. Error in checkbook whereby a check for $181 was entered into the checkbook as $118

Exercise 4 (LO 2) PREPARE JOURNAL ENTRIES FOR BANK RECONCILIATION

Based on the following bank reconciliation, prepare the necessary journal entries as of January 28, 20--:

Bank statement balance, January 28		$1,896.00
Add: Deposits in transit:		
1/26	$118.00	
1/28	92.00	210.00
		$2,106.00
Deduct: Outstanding checks:		
No. 683	$ 23.00	
No. 685	6.50	
No. 687	102.50	
No. 688	13.00	
No. 689	208.00	353.00
Adjusted bank balance		$1,753.00
Book balance, January 28		$1,994.00
Add: Error on check*	$ 28.00	
Note collected**	142.00	170.00
		$2,164.00
Deduct: Unrecorded ATM withdrawal***	$ 30.00	
Service charge	11.00	
NSF check	370.00	411.00
Adjusted book balance		$1,753.00

  *Accounts Payable was debited.
 **Credit Notes Receivable.
***Debit Gail Bennett, Drawing.

Exercise 4 (Concluded)

GENERAL JOURNAL   PAGE

	DATE		DESCRIPTION	POST. REF.	DEBIT	CREDIT	
1							1
2							2
3							3
4							4
5							5
6							6
7							7
8							8
9							9
10							10
11							11
12							12
13							13
14							14
15							15
16							16
17							17
18							18
19							19
20							20
21							21
22							22

Exercise 5 (LO3) PETTY CASH JOURNAL ENTRIES

Based on the following petty cash information, prepare journal entries to establish the petty cash fund and to replenish the fund at the end of the month.

1. On March 1, a check is written for $100 to establish a petty cash fund.

2. During the month, the following petty cash payments are made:

Phone Expense	$ 3.50
Automobile Expense	11.00
Postage Expense	4.50
B. Crenshaw, Drawing	35.00
Charitable Contributions Expense	25.00
Miscellaneous Expense	3.00

Exercise 5 (Concluded)

GENERAL JOURNAL PAGE 1

	DATE	DESCRIPTION	POST. REF.	DEBIT	CREDIT	
1						1
2						2
3						3
4						4
5						5
6						6
7						7
8						8
9						9
10						10
11						11
12						12

Exercise 6 (LO4) CASH SHORT AND OVER JOURNAL ENTRIES

Based on the following information, prepare weekly entries for cash receipts from service fees and cash short and over. A change fund of $100 is maintained.

Aug.	5	Cash in drawer:	$318.00	Cash register amount:	$218.00
	12		402.00		300.00
	19		388.00		292.00
	26		411.50		309.50

Exercise 6 (Concluded)

GENERAL JOURNAL

	DATE		DESCRIPTION	POST. REF.	DEBIT	CREDIT	
1							1
2							2
3							3
4							4
5							5
6							6
7							7
8							8
9							9
10							10
11							11
12							12
13							13
14							14
15							15
16							16
17							17
18							18
19							19

PROBLEMS

Problem 7 (LO2) BANK RECONCILIATION AND RELATED JOURNAL ENTRIES

The following information relates to the bank account of the Mini Donut House:

Balance, March 31, per check stub		$2,923
Balance, March 31, per bank statement		3,199
March deposits not shown on bank statement	$302	
	206	508
Bank service charge shown on bank statement		14
Unrecorded ATM withdrawal*		60
NSF check shown on bank statement		153

Error on Check No. 144, where stub shows $132, but the check was made in the amount of $123. Accounts Payable was originally debited.

Checks outstanding, March 31, are as follows:

No. 148	$201.00
No. 151	300.00
No. 155	501.00

*Funds were withdrawn by the owner, Paolo Goes, for personal use.

Required:

1. Prepare the bank reconciliation.
2. Prepare the required journal entries.

Problem 7 (Continued)

1.

Problem 7 (Concluded)

2.

GENERAL JOURNAL   PAGE 1

	DATE		DESCRIPTION	POST. REF.	DEBIT	CREDIT	
1							1
2							2
3							3
4							4
5							5
6							6
7							7
8							8
9							9
10							10
11							11
12							12
13							13
14							14
15							15
16							16
17							17
18							18
19							19
20							20
21							21
22							22
23							23
24							24
25							25
26							26
27							27
28							28
29							29

Problem 8 (LO3) PETTY CASH PAYMENTS RECORD AND JOURNAL ENTRIES

On April 1, the Fitzgibbons Furniture Repair Shop established a petty cash fund of $200. The following cash payments were made from the petty cash fund during the first two weeks of April. The fund was replenished to the $200 level on April 16.

Apr.	1	Paid $5.28 for postage due on a package received. Petty Cash Voucher No. 10.
	5	Made a $25 contribution to the Washington Township Baseball League. Petty Cash Voucher No. 11.
	6	Reimbursed $6.25 to an employee for phone calls made from a pay phone. Petty Cash Voucher No. 12.
	8	Paid $22 for office supplies. Petty Cash Voucher No. 13.
	10	Paid $32 for a newspaper advertisement. Petty Cash Voucher No. 14.
	12	Paid $33 for an oil change for the company truck. Petty Cash Voucher No. 15.
	14	Paid $20 for postage stamps. Petty Cash Voucher No. 16.
	15	Made a $25 contribution to the Girl Scouts. Petty Cash Voucher No. 17.

Required:

1. Prepare the journal entry to establish the petty cash fund.
2. Enter the above payments in the petty cash payments record provided on page 113.
3. Prove the petty cash payments record.
4. Prepare the journal entry to replenish the fund on April 16.

**Problem 8 (Continued)
2. and 3.**

PETTY CASH PAYMENTS FOR MONTH OF

PAGE 1

20--

DAY	DESCRIPTION	VOU. NO.	TOTAL AMOUNT	DISTRIBUTION OF PAYMENTS							ACCOUNT	AMOUNT
				TRUCK EXPENSE	POSTAGE EXPENSE	CHARIT. CONTRIB. EXPENSE	PHONE EXPENSE	OFFICE SUPPLIES	ADVERT. EXPENSE			
1												
2												
3												
4												
5												
6												
7												
8												
9												
10												
11												
12												
13												
14												
15												
16												
17												
18												
19												
20												
21												
22												

Problem 8 (Concluded)
1. and 4.

GENERAL JOURNAL   PAGE   1

	DATE	DESCRIPTION	POST. REF.	DEBIT	CREDIT	
1						1
2						2
3						3
4						4
5						5
6						6
7						7
8						8
9						9
10						10
11						11
12						12

Problem 9 (LO4) CASH SHORT AND OVER JOURNAL ENTRIES

Mackie's Salon deposits cash weekly. A record of cash register receipts for the month of April is shown below. A change fund of $100 is maintained.

Apr.					
	2	Cash in drawer:	$298.00	Cash register amount:	$196.50
	9		286.50		192.00
	16		293.50		193.50
	23		306.00		204.50
	30		301.50		203.00

Required:

Prepare weekly journal entries for cash receipts from service fees, showing cash short and over when needed.

Problem 9 (Concluded)

GENERAL JOURNAL

PAGE 1

	DATE		DESCRIPTION	POST. REF.	DEBIT	CREDIT	
1							1
2							2
3							3
4							4
5							5
6							6
7							7
8							8
9							9
10							10
11							11
12							12
13							13
14							14
15							15
16							16
17							17
18							18
19							19
20							20
21							21
22							22
23							23
24							24
25							25
26							26
27							27
28							28
29							29
30							30
31							31
32							32

CHAPTER 8
PAYROLL ACCOUNTING:
EMPLOYEE EARNINGS AND DEDUCTIONS

LEARNING OBJECTIVES

Payroll accounting is an important part of any business, partly because it is such a significant expense and partly because so many laws govern its record keeping. In Chapter 8, we examine the payroll records that employers are required to keep and also those records that help run the business efficiently.

Objective 1.   Distinguish between employees and independent contractors.

An **employee** is one who works under the control and direction of an employer. The employer controls how and when the job is to be done, determines working hours, and in general is responsible for all aspects of the employee's work. An **independent contractor**, on the other hand, performs a service for a fee and does not work under the control and direction of the company paying for his or her service. This is an important distinction because employers are required to maintain payroll records and file many reports for their employees but must file only one form for independent contractors.

Objective 2.   Calculate employee earnings and deductions.

Three steps are required to determine how much to pay an employee for a pay period. (1) Calculate the employee's total earnings for the pay period. (2) Determine the amounts of deductions for the same pay period. (3) Subtract deductions from total earnings. The deductions may be required by law—for example, Social Security and Medicare taxes and federal and state income taxes—or by agreement with the employer—for example, insurance deductions and savings bond deductions.

Objective 3.   Describe and prepare payroll records.

Three types of payroll records are used to accumulate required information for federal and state tax purposes: the payroll register, the payroll check (or record of direct deposit) with earnings statement attached, and the employee earnings record.

The **payroll register** is a multi-column form that accumulates the necessary data to prepare the journal entry. Detailed information on earnings, taxable earnings, deductions, and net pay is provided for each employee and for the employees in total.

The **payroll check** (or record of direct deposit) is prepared from information in the payroll register. The detachable earnings statement attached to the employee's check shows the gross earnings, total deductions, and net pay.

A separate record of each employee's earnings is called an **employee earnings record.** This information is also obtained from the payroll register. The earnings record is designed so that quarterly and annual totals can be accumulated in order for the employer to prepare several reports.

Objective 4.   Account for employee earnings and deductions.

The payroll register provides all the information needed to prepare the journal entry for any pay period. The total gross earnings is debited to a wages and salaries expense account, and each deduction is credited to a current liability account. The difference between gross earnings and total deductions is called **net pay** and is credited to Cash.

Objective 5.   Describe various payroll record-keeping methods.

In addition to a manual system of preparing all the necessary payroll records, payroll processing centers and electronic systems can be used to prepare the same records.

A **payroll processing center** is a business that sells payroll record-keeping services. An **electronic system** is a computer system based on a software package that performs all payroll record keeping and prepares payroll checks or EFTs.

REVIEW QUESTIONS

Instructions: Analyze each of the following items carefully before writing your answer in the column at the right.

Question	Answer
Question	**Answer**

LO 1   1. A(n) _____ is one who works under the control and direction of an employer. ....

LO 1   2. A(n) _____ performs a service for a fee and does not work under the control and direction of the company paying for the service. ....

LO 2   3. What three steps are required to determine how much to pay an employee for a pay period? ....

LO 2   4. Compensation for managerial or administrative services, normally expressed in biweekly, monthly, or annual terms, is called _____.

LO 2   5. Compensation for skilled or unskilled labor, normally expressed in terms of hours, weeks, or units produced, is called _____. ....

LO 2   6. When compensation is based on time, _____ are helpful for keeping a record of the time worked by each employee. ....

LO 2   7. An employee's total earnings is also called _____. ....

LO 2   8. An employee's total earnings less all the deductions is called _____.

LO 2   9. What are the three major categories of deductions from an employee's paycheck? ....

LO 2   10. David Astin is married with two children, holds only one job, and has a spouse who is not employed. What number of withholding allowances is Astin entitled to claim, assuming that he does not anticipate large itemized deductions? ....

LO 2 11. Upon employment, each employee is required to furnish the employer a Form _____ that details, among other things, the number of withholding allowances and marital status. .... _____

LO 2 12. Name the four factors that determine the amount to be withheld from an employee's gross pay each pay period. .... _____

_____

_____

_____

LO 3 13. A form used to assemble the data required at the end of each payroll period is called a(n) _____. .... _____

LO 3 14. A method of payment in which the employee's net pay is placed directly in the employee's bank account is called a(n) _____. ..... _____

LO 3 15. A separate, detailed record of each employee's earnings is called a(n) _____ . ... _____

LO 5 16. Name two approaches in addition to a manual system used to accumulate and record payroll information. .... _____

_____

EXERCISES

Exercise 1 (LO 2) COMPUTING OVERTIME PAY RATE

Lu-yin Cheng receives a regular salary of $2,500 a month and is entitled to overtime pay at the rate of 1½ times the regular hourly rate for any time worked in excess of 40 hours per week. Compute Cheng's overtime hourly rate.

_____

_____

_____

_____

_____

_____

_____

_____

_____

_____

Exercise 2 (LO 2) COMPUTING GROSS PAY

Roger Watkins earns a regular hourly rate of $12.50 and receives time and a half for any time worked over 8 hours per weekday. Roger earns double time for hours worked on Saturday or Sunday. During the past week, Roger worked 8 hours each day Monday through Wednesday, 5 hours on Thursday, 12 hours on Friday, and 6 hours on Saturday. Compute Watkins's gross pay.

_____

_____

_____

_____

_____

_____

_____

_____

_____

Exercise 3 (LO 2) COMPUTING NET PAY

Bill Burry is married, has three children, and claims five withholding allowances for federal income tax purposes. Burry's gross pay for the week was $683. Using the federal income tax withholding tables provided in Figure 8-4 of the text and the information provided below, compute Burry's net pay for the week.

(a) Social Security tax rate is 6.2% (Burry's prior earnings equaled $23,455).
(b) Medicare tax rate is 1.45%.
(c) State income tax is 2% of gross earnings.
(d) City income tax is 1% of gross earnings.
(e) Contribution to pension plan is $25.
(f) Health insurance deduction is $8.50.

_____

_____

_____

_____

_____

_____

_____

_____

_____

_____

Exercise 4 (LO 4) JOURNALIZING PAYROLL TRANSACTIONS

Using the information provided in Exercise 3, enter the payment of Bill Burry's wages in a general journal. Assume a pay period ending on July 31, 20--.

GENERAL JOURNAL   PAGE 1

	DATE		DESCRIPTION	POST. REF.	DEBIT	CREDIT	
1							1
2							2
3							3
4							4
5							5
6							6
7							7
8							8
9							9
10							10

Exercise 5 (LO 3, 4) PAYROLL JOURNAL ENTRIES

The following data were taken from the payroll register of United Processors as of May 14, 20--.

Regular earnings	$6,516.00
Overtime earnings	710.00
Total earnings	_____
Deductions:	
Federal income tax	_____
Social Security tax	448.01
Medicare tax	104.78
Pension plan	134.00
Health insurance	260.00
United Way	190.00
Net pay	$5,394.21

Required:

1. Determine the missing amounts.
2. Prepare the journal entry for the payroll, crediting Cash for the net pay.

1.

_____

_____

_____

_____

Exercise 5 (Concluded)

2.

GENERAL JOURNAL   PAGE

	DATE		DESCRIPTION	POST. REF.	DEBIT	CREDIT	
1							1
2							2
3							3
4							4
5							5
6							6
7							7
8							8
9							9
10							10
11							11
12							12

PROBLEMS

Problem 6 (LO 2, 3, 4) PAYROLL REGISTER AND PAYROLL JOURNAL ENTRIES

Earl Wilson operates a business known as Wilson Enterprises. Listed below are the name, number of allowances claimed, marital status, total hours worked, and hourly rate of each employee. All hours worked in excess of 40 a week are paid for at the rate of time and a half.

The employer uses a weekly federal income tax withholding table. A portion of this weekly table is provided in Chapter 8 of your textbook. Social Security tax is withheld at the rate of 6.2%, Medicare tax is withheld at the rate of 1.45%, state income tax is withheld at the rate of 3.5%, and city earnings tax is withheld at the rate of 1%. Kagan, Kennedy, Scalia, and Sotomayor each have $15 withheld this payday for group life insurance. Each employee, except Ginsberg, has $5 withheld for health insurance. All of the employees use payroll deduction to the credit union for varying amounts as listed below. Alito, Kennedy, and Thomas each have $18.25 withheld this payday under a savings bond purchase plan.

Wilson Enterprises follows the practice of drawing a single check for the net amount of the payroll and depositing the check in a special payroll account at the bank. Individual paychecks are then drawn for the amount due each employee. The checks issued this payday were numbered consecutively beginning with Check No. 531.

Wilson Enterprises
Payroll Information for the Week Ended January 15, 20--

Name	Allow-ances	Marital Status	Total Hours Worked	Regular Hourly Rate	Credit Union Deposit	Cumul. Earnings thru 1/8
Alito, Samuel	3	M	45	$12.00	$114.00	$525.00
Breyer, Susan	2	M	50	10.00	110.00	680.00
Ginsberg, Ruth	3	M	43	11.00	97.90	500.00
Kagan, Ellen	2	S	48	11.00	114.40	625.00
Kennedy, Tony	3	M	43	13.00	115.70	730.00
Roberts, John	5	M	40	17.00	136.00	850.00
Scalia, Anton	2	S	38	9.00	68.40	425.00
Sotomayor, Sonja	4	M	47	11.00	111.10	635.00
Thomas, Clarence	1	S	60	10.00	140.00	615.00

Required:

1. Prepare a payroll register for Wilson Enterprises for the pay period ended January 15, 20--. Use the form provided on pages 124–125. (In the Taxable Earnings/Unemployment Compensation column, enter the same amounts as in the Social Security column.)

2. Assuming that the wages for the week ended January 15 were paid on January 17, enter the payment in the general journal provided on page 125.

Problem 6 (Continued)

1.

PAYROLL REGISTER

	NAME	EMP. NO.	NO. ALLOW.	MARIT. STATUS	EARNINGS								TAXABLE EARNINGS			
					REGULAR		OVERTIME		TOTAL		CUMULATIVE TOTAL		UNEMPLOY. COMP.		SOCIAL SECURITY	
1																
2																
3																
4																
5																
6																
7																
8																
9																
10																
11																
12																
13																
14																

Problem 6 (Concluded)

FOR PERIOD ENDED   20--

							DEDUCTIONS					
FEDERAL INC. TAX	SOC. SEC. TAX	MEDICARE TAX	STATE INC. TAX	CITY EARN. TAX	LIFE INS.	HEALTH INS.	CREDIT UNION	OTHER	TOTAL	NET PAY	CK. NO.	
												1
												2
												3
												4
												5
												6
												7
												8
												9
												10
												11
												12
												13
												14

2.

GENERAL JOURNAL   PAGE 1

	DATE	DESCRIPTION	POST. REF.	DEBIT	CREDIT	
1						1
2						2
3						3
4						4
5						5
6						6
7						7
8						8
9						9
10						10
11						11
12						12
13						13

Problem 7 (LO 3) EMPLOYEE EARNINGS RECORD

The current employee earnings record for Susan Breyer is provided below and on page 127. Using the information provided in Problem 6, update Breyer's earnings record to reflect the January 15 payroll. Although this information should have been entered earlier, complete the required information at the bottom of the earnings record. The necessary information is provided below.

Name:	Susan Breyer
Address:	422 Long Plain Rd.
	Leverett, MA 01054
Employee No.:	2
Gender:	Female
Department:	Sanitation
Occupation:	Janitor
S.S. No.:	336-56-7534
Marital Status:	Married
Allowances:	4
Pay Rate:	$10 per hour
Birth Date:	7/6/69
Date Employed:	6/22/--

EMPLOYEE EARNINGS RECORD

20 -- PERIOD ENDED	EARNINGS							TAXABLE EARNINGS				DEDUCTIONS			
	REGULAR		OVERTIME		TOTAL		CUMULATIVE TOTAL	UNEMPLOY. COMP.		SOCIAL SECURITY		FEDERAL INCOME TAX		SOCIAL SECURITY TAX	
Jan. 1	300	00			300	00	300	00	300	00	300	00	0	00	18	60
8	380	00			380	00	680	00	380	00	380	00	7	00	23	56

GENDER		DEPARTMENT	OCCUPATION	SOCIAL SECURITY NO.	MARITAL STATUS	ALLOW-ANCES
M	F					

Problem 7 (Concluded)

FOR PERIOD ENDED　　　　　　　　　　　　　　　　　　　　20--

DEDUCTIONS																
MEDICARE TAX		STATE INCOME TAX		CITY EARNINGS TAX		LIFE INSUR.		HEALTH INSUR.		CREDIT UNION		OTHER		TOTAL		NET PAY		CK. NO.
4	35	10	50	3	00			5	00	40	00			81	45	218	55	321
5	51	13	30	3	80			5	00	56	00			114	17	265	83	422

PAY RATE	DATE OF BIRTH	DATE HIRED	NAME/ADDRESS	EMP. NO.

CHAPTER 9
PAYROLL ACCOUNTING: EMPLOYER TAXES AND REPORTS

LEARNING OBJECTIVES

Chapter 8 discussed taxes levied on the employee and withheld by the employer. None of these taxes was an expense of the employer. In Chapter 9, we examine several taxes that represent an additional payroll expense imposed directly on the employer.

Objective 1.   Describe and calculate employer payroll taxes.

Most employers are subject to a matching portion of the Social Security and Medicare taxes and to federal and state unemployment taxes. The employer's **Social Security and Medicare taxes** are levied on employers at the same rates and on the same bases as the employee Social Security and Medicare taxes. The **FUTA** tax is levied only on employers. The purpose of this tax is to raise funds to administer the federal/state unemployment compensation program. The **SUTA** tax is also levied only on employers. The purpose of this tax is to raise funds to pay unemployment benefits.

The Social Security, FUTA, and SUTA taxes are calculated from the accumulated amounts found in the Taxable Earnings columns in the payroll register. The Medicare tax is calculated from the Earnings—Total column.

Objective 2.   Account for employer payroll taxes expense.

To journalize employer payroll taxes, debit the total of the employer Social Security, Medicare, FUTA, and SUTA taxes to a single account entitled Payroll Taxes Expense. The liabilities for the Social Security, Medicare, FUTA, and SUTA taxes payable normally are credited to separate accounts. The general format of this entry appears below.

Payroll Taxes Expense	xx	
Social Security Tax Payable		xx
Medicare Tax Payable		xx
FUTA Tax Payable		xx
SUTA Tax Payable		xx

Objective 3.   Describe employer reporting and payment responsibilities.

Employer payroll reporting and payment responsibilities fall in six areas.

1. Federal income tax withholding and Social Security and Medicare taxes
2. FUTA taxes
3. SUTA taxes
4. Employee Wage and Tax Statement (Form W-2)
5. Summary of employee wages and taxes (Form W-3)
6. Employment eligibility notification (Form I-9)

The due date for federal income tax withholding and Social Security and Medicare taxes varies, depending on the amount of these taxes. Deposits are made using EFTPS. In addition, a Form 941 must be completed each quarter and filed with the IRS.

The federal unemployment taxes must be computed on a quarterly basis. In addition, Form 940 must be filed with the IRS by the beginning of the second week of February.

Deposit rules and forms for state unemployment taxes vary among the states. Deposits usually are required on a quarterly basis.

Employers must furnish each employee with a Wage and Tax Statement (Form W-2) by January 31 of each year. Information needed to complete this form is contained in the employee earnings records. The employer also must file Form W-3 with the Social Security Administration by the last day of February. This form summarizes the employee earnings and tax information from Forms W-2.

The purpose of Form I-9 is to document that each employee is authorized to work in the United States. It must be completed by the employee and employer and retained by the employer.

Objective 4.   Describe and account for workers' compensation insurance.

Workers' compensation insurance provides insurance for employees who suffer a work-related illness or injury. The cost of the insurance depends on the number of employees, the riskiness of the job, and the company's accident history. The employer usually pays the premium at the beginning of the year, based on the estimated annual payroll, and makes an adjustment at the end of the year when the actual annual payroll is known.

REVIEW QUESTIONS

Instructions: Analyze each of the following items carefully before writing your answer in the column at the right.

Question	Answer
LO 1 **1.** Name the four payroll taxes paid by the employer.	_____
	_____
	_____
	_____
LO 1 **2.** The textbook uses a Social Security tax rate of 6.2% applied to maximum employee earnings of _____.	_____
LO 1 **3.** The _____ is a key source of information for computing employer payroll taxes.	_____
LO 1 **4.** Individuals who own and run their own business are considered ____.	_____
LO 1 **5.** The law requires persons earning net self-employment income of $400 or more to pay a(n) _____.	_____
LO 1 **6.** The textbook uses a FUTA tax rate of 0.6% applied to maximum employee earnings of _____.	_____
LO 2 **7.** When journalizing the employer's payroll taxes, debit the total of the employer Social Security, Medicare, FUTA, and SUTA taxes to a single account entitled _____.	_____
LO 3 **8.** Name the three taxes that are associated with Form 941.	_____
	_____
	_____
LO 3 **9.** In addition to making quarterly deposits, employers are required to file an annual report of federal unemployment tax on Form _____.	_____

LO 3 10. By January 31 of each year, employers must furnish each employee
with a(n) _____. ....   _____

LO 3 11. _____ documents that an employee is authorized to work in the
United States. ....   _____

LO 4 12. _____ provides insurance for employees who suffer a work-related
illness or injury. ....   _____

EXERCISES

Exercise 1 (LO 1) CALCULATION OF EMPLOYER PAYROLL TAXES

Sylvania Bookstore pays a SUTA tax of 5.4% and a FUTA tax of 0.6%. The total taxable wages for unemployment compensation on a certain payday amount to $16,800. Compute the unemployment taxes payable to the state and federal government.

_____

_____

_____

_____

_____

_____

_____

_____

_____

_____

_____

Exercise 2 (LO 2) CALCULATION OF PAYROLL TAXES AND PREPARATION OF JOURNAL ENTRIES

The Totals line from Wong Drug Store's payroll register for the week ended December 31, 20--, is shown on pages 132 and 133.

Payroll taxes are imposed as follows:

Social Security tax   6.2%
Medicare tax   1.45%
FUTA tax   0.6%
SUTA tax   5.4%

Required:

1. Prepare the journal entry for payment of this payroll on December 31, 20--.
2. Prepare the journal entry for the employer's payroll taxes for the period ended December 31, 20--.

Exercise 2 (Continued)

PAYROLL REGISTER

	NAME	EMPL. NO.	NO. ALLOW.	MARIT. STATUS	EARNINGS						TAXABLE EARNINGS			
					REGULAR		OVERTIME		TOTAL		CUMULATIVE TOTAL		UNEMPLOY. COMP.		SOCIAL SECURITY	
1	Totals				4,200	00	500	00	4,700	00	203,700	00	300	00	3,600	00
2																
3																
4																
5																
6																
7																
8																
9																
10																

1. and 2.

GENERAL JOURNAL   PAGE 1

	DATE		DESCRIPTION	POST. REF.	DEBIT	CREDIT	
1							1
2							2
3							3
4							4
5							5
6							6
7							7
8							8
9							9
10							10
11							11
12							12
13							13
14							14
15							15
16							16

Exercise 2 (Concluded)

FOR PERIOD ENDED   December 31, 20--

DEDUCTIONS																	
FEDERAL INC. TAX		SOC. SEC. TAX		MEDICARE TAX		HEALTH INS.		CREDIT UNION		OTHER			TOTAL		NET PAY		CK. NO.	
420	00	223	20	68	15	80	00	200	00				991	35	3,708	65		1
																		2
																		3
																		4
																		5
																		6
																		7
																		8
																		9
																		10

Exercise 3 (LO1/2) TOTAL COST OF AN EMPLOYEE

Compute the total annual cost to an employer of employing a person whose gross salary is $45,000. (Assume a 5.4% state unemployment tax rate and a FUTA tax rate of 0.6%, both on the first $7,000 of earnings, an employer's Social Security tax rate of 6.2% on the first $118,500 of earnings and a Medicare tax rate of 1.45% on gross earnings.)

_____

_____

_____

_____

_____

_____

_____

_____

Exercise 4 (LO 3) JOURNAL ENTRIES FOR PAYMENT OF PAYROLL TAXES

The general ledger of GNU Co. includes the following accounts and balances related to payroll as of October 15 of the current year:

Social Security Tax Payable	$12,400
Medicare Tax Payable	2,900
FUTA Tax Payable	540
SUTA Tax Payable	4,320
Employee Federal Income Tax Payable	7,780

Required:

Journalize the payment of the employee federal income taxes and Social Security and Medicare taxes on October 15, 20--, and the deposit of the FUTA and SUTA taxes on October 31, 20--.

GENERAL JOURNAL   PAGE

	DATE		DESCRIPTION	POST. REF.	DEBIT	CREDIT	
1							1
2							2
3							3
4							4
5							5
6							6
7							7
8							8
9							9
10							10
11							11
12							12
13							13
14							14

Exercise 5 (LO 4) WORKERS' COMPENSATION INSURANCE AND ADJUSTMENT

Curtis Company paid a premium of $360 for workers' compensation insurance based on the estimated payroll as of the beginning of the year. Based on actual payroll as of the end of the year, the actual premium is $397. Prepare the adjusting entry to reflect the underpayment of the insurance premium.

GENERAL JOURNAL

PAGE 1

	DATE	DESCRIPTION	POST. REF.	DEBIT	CREDIT	
1						1
2						2
3						3
4						4
5						5

PROBLEMS

Problem 6 (LO 1/2) CALCULATING PAYROLL TAXES EXPENSE AND PREPARING JOURNAL ENTRY

A partial payroll register for the pay period ended August 31, 20--, is provided on the following page for the Astroscope Company.

Required:

1. Compute the total earnings subject to federal and state unemployment taxes and the Social Security tax by completing the Taxable Earnings columns of the payroll register.

2. Assume the company is in a state with an unemployment tax rate of 5.4% and a FUTA tax rate of 0.6%, both on the first $7,000 of earnings. The Social Security tax rate is 6.2% on the first $118,500 of earnings, and the Medicare tax rate is 1.45% on gross earnings. Compute the state and federal unemployment taxes and the Social Security and Medicare taxes on the lines provided on page 136.

3. Prepare the entry for the employer's payroll taxes in the general journal provided on page 137.

Problem 6 (Continued)

1.

PAYROLL REGISTER

	NAME	NO. ALLOW.	MARIT. STATUS	EARNINGS				TAXABLE EARNINGS	
				REGULAR	OVERTIME	TOTAL	CUMULATIVE TOTAL	UNEMPLOY. COMP.	SOCIAL SECURITY
1	Coolie, Betty					350 00	7,150 00		
2	Covar, Mike					200 00	6,800 00		
3	Hagen, Frank					375 00	6,200 00		
4	Gutierrez, Bob					1,540 00	47,300 00		
5	Moten, Alice					1,500 00	50,500 00		
6	Rice, Darlene					3,300 00	121,400 00		
7									

2.

Problem 6 (Concluded)

3.

GENERAL JOURNAL   PAGE   1

	DATE	DESCRIPTION	POST. REF.	DEBIT	CREDIT	
1						1
2						2
3						3
4						4
5						5
6						6
7						7
8						8
9						9

Problem 7 (LO 2/3) JOURNALIZING AND POSTING PAYROLL ENTRIES

Rock Creek Company has five employees. All are paid on a monthly basis. The fiscal year of the business is March 1 to February 28. Payroll taxes are imposed as follows:

Social Security tax to be withheld from employees' wages and imposed on the employer, 6.2% each on the first $118,500 of earnings.

Medicare tax to be withheld from employees' wages and imposed on the employer, 1.45% each on gross earnings.

SUTA tax imposed on the employer, 5.4% on the first $7,000 of earnings.

FUTA tax imposed on the employer, 0.6% on the first $7,000 of earnings.

The accounts kept by Rock Creek Company include the following:

Account Number	Title	Balance on March 1
101	Cash	$62,500.00
211	Employee Federal Income Tax Payable	3,375.00
212	Social Security Tax Payable	4,740.00
213	Medicare Tax Payable	1,110.00
218	Savings Bond Deductions Payable	1,200.00
221	FUTA Tax Payable	320.00
222	SUTA Tax Payable	2,670.00
511	Wages and Salaries Expense	0.00
530	Payroll Taxes Expense	0.00

Problem 7 (Continued)

Following is a narrative of selected transactions relating to payrolls and payroll taxes that occurred during the months of March and April:

Mar.	15	Paid $9,225.00 covering the following February taxes:		
		Employee federal income tax withheld		$3,375.00
		Social Security tax		4,740.00
		Medicare tax		1,110.00
		Total		$9,225.00
	31	March payroll:		
		Total wages and salaries expense		$39,000.00
		Less amounts withheld:		
		Employee federal income tax	$3,690.00	
		Social Security tax	2,418.00	
		Medicare tax	565.50	
		Savings bond deductions payable	1,200.00	7,873.50
		Net amount paid		$31,126.50
	31	Purchased savings bonds for employees, $2,400.00		
	31	Data for completing employer's payroll taxes expense for March:		
		Social Security taxable wages		$39,000.00
		Unemployment taxable wages		12,000.00
Apr.	15	Paid $9,657.00 covering the following March taxes:		
		Employee federal income tax payable		$ 3,690.00
		Social Security tax		4,836.00
		Medicare tax		1,131.00
	30	Paid SUTA tax for the quarter, $3,318.00		
	30	Paid FUTA tax, $392.00		

Required:

1. Using a general journal, journalize the preceding transactions.
2. Open T accounts for the payroll expense and liabilities. Enter the beginning balances and post the transactions recorded in the journal.

Problem 7 (Continued)

1.

GENERAL JOURNAL   PAGE _____

	DATE	DESCRIPTION	POST. REF.	DEBIT	CREDIT	
1						1
2						2
3						3
4						4
5						5
6						6
7						7
8						8
9						9
10						10
11						11
12						12
13						13
14						14
15						15
16						16
17						17
18						18
19						19
20						20
21						21
22						22
23						23
24						24
25						25
26						26
27						27
28						28
29						29
30						30

Problem 7 (Continued)

GENERAL JOURNAL

	DATE	DESCRIPTION	POST. REF.	DEBIT	CREDIT	
1						1
2						2
3						3
4						4
5						5
6						6
7						7
8						8
9						9
10						10
11						11
12						12
13						13
14						14

2.

Cash   101

Employee Federal Income Tax Payable   211

Social Security Tax Payable   212

Medicare Tax Payable   213

Problem 7 (Concluded)

Savings Bond Deductions Payable 218	FUTA Tax Payable 221

SUTA Tax Payable 222	Wages and Salaries Expense 511

Payroll Taxes Expense   530

Problem 8 (LO 4) WORKERS' COMPENSATION INSURANCE AND ADJUSTMENT

Jackson Manufacturing estimated its total payroll for the coming year to be $630,000. The workers' compensation insurance premium rate is 0.35%.

Required:

1. Calculate the estimated workers' compensation insurance premium and prepare the journal entry for the payment as of January 2, 20--.

2. Assume Jackson Manufacturing's actual payroll for the year is $658,000. Calculate the total insurance premium owed. Prepare a journal entry as of December 31, 20--, to record the adjustment for the underpayment. The actual payment of the additional insurance premium will take place in January of the next year.

3. Assume, instead, that Jackson Manufacturing's actual payroll for the year is $607,000. Prepare a journal entry as of December 31, 20--, for the total amount that should be refunded. The refund will not be received until the next year.

1., 2., and 3.

GENERAL JOURNAL

PAGE 1

	DATE	DESCRIPTION	POST. REF.	DEBIT	CREDIT	
1						1
2						2
3						3
4						4
5						5
6						6
7						7
8						8
9						9
10						10
11						11
12						12
13						13
14						14

NOTES

NOTES

NOTES

NOTES

NOTES

NOTES

NOTES

NOTES

NOTES

NOTES

NOTES

NOTES

NOTES

END PAGE OF

STUDY GUIDE

Working Papers

Chapters 1-9

College Accounting

Twenty-second Edition

James A. Heintz, DBA, CPA
Professor of Accounting
School of Business
University of Kansas

Robert W. Parry, Jr., Ph.D.
Professor of Accounting
Kelley School of Business
Indiana University

Australia • Brazil • Mexico • Singapore • United Kingdom • United States

ISBN: 978-1-305-66767-9

Cengage Learning
20 Channel Center Street
Boston, MA 02210
USA

Cengage Learning is a leading provider of customized learning solutions with employees residing in nearly 40 different countries and sales in more than 125 countries around the world. Find your local representative at **www.cengage.com**.

Cengage Learning products are represented in Canada by Nelson Education, Ltd.

To learn more about Cengage Learning Solutions, visit **www.cengage.com**.

Purchase any of our products at your local college store or at our preferred online store **www.cengagebrain.com**.

Printed in the United States of America
Print Number: 01   Print Year: 2015

Table of Contents

Exercise 1-1A

1. _____ Owners

2. _____ Managers

3. _____ Creditors

4. _____ Government agencies

a. Whether the firm can pay its bills on time

b. Detailed, up-to-date information to measure business performance (and plan for future operations)

c. To determine taxes to be paid and whether other regulations are met

d. The firm's current financial condition

Exercise 1-2A

Order	Accounting Process	Definition
_____	Recording	_____
		_____
		_____
_____	Summarizing	_____
		_____
		_____
_____	Reporting	_____
		_____
		_____
_____	Analyzing	_____
		_____
		_____
_____	Interpreting	_____
		_____
		_____
_____	Classifying	_____
		_____
		_____

Exercise 1-1B

Users	Information
Owners (present and future):	_____
	_____
	_____
Managers:	_____
	_____
	_____
Creditors (present and future):	_____
	_____
	_____
Government agencies:	_____
	_____
	_____

Exercise 1-2B

Letter	Accounting Process		Definition
_____	Analyzing	a.	Telling the results
_____	Recording	b.	Looking at events that have taken place and thinking about how they affect the business
_____	Classifying		
_____	Summarizing	c.	Deciding the importance of the various reports
_____	Reporting	d.	Aggregating many similar events to provide information that is easy to understand
_____	Interpreting		
		e.	Sorting and grouping like items together
		f.	Entering financial information into the accounting system

Exercise 2-1A

Item	Account	Classification
Money in bank	Cash	_____
Office supplies	Supplies	_____
Money owed	Accounts Payable	_____
Office chairs	Office Furniture	_____
Net worth of owner	John Smith, Capital	_____
Money withdrawn by owner	John Smith, Drawing	_____
Money owed by customers	Accounts Receivable	_____

Exercise 2-2A

Assets	=	Liabilities	+	Owner's Equity
_____	=	$27,000	+	$17,000
$32,000	=	$18,000	+	_____
$27,000	=	_____	+	$20,000

Exercise 2-3A

	Assets	=	Liabilities	+	Owner's Equity
(a)	_____		_____		_____
Bal.	_____		_____		_____
(b)	_____		_____		_____
Bal.	_____		_____		_____
(c)	_____		_____		_____
	_____		_____		_____
Bal.	_____		_____		_____
(d)	_____		_____		_____
Bal.	_____		_____		_____

Exercise 2-4A

	Assets	=	Liabilities	+	Capital	−	Drawing	+	Revenues	−	Expenses	Description
						Owner's Equity						
Bal. from E 2-3A												
(d)												
(e)												
(f)												
(g)												
(h)												
(i)												
(j)												
(k)												
Bal.												

Exercise 2-5A

Account	Classification	Financial Statement
Cash	_____	_____
Rent Expense	_____	_____
Accounts Payable	_____	_____
Service Fees	_____	_____
Supplies	_____	_____
Wages Expense	_____	_____
Ramon Martinez, Drawing	_____	_____
Ramon Martinez, Capital	_____	_____
Prepaid Insurance	_____	_____
Accounts Receivable	_____	_____

Exercise 2-6A

Exercise 2-7A

Problem 2-8A

	Assets	=	Liabilities	+	Owner's Equity
1.	_____		_____		_____
2.	_____		_____		_____
3.	_____		_____		_____

Problem 2-9A: See page WP-7

Problem 2-10A

Problem 2-9A

Cash	+	Accounts Receivable	+	Office Supplies	+	Prepaid Insurance	=	Accounts Payable	+	J. Pembroke, Capital	–	J. Pembroke, Drawing	+	Revenues	–	Expenses	Description

Assets = Liabilities + Owner's Equity

(Items Owned) — (Amts. Owed) — (Owner's Investment) — (Earnings)

(a)
(b)
(c)
(d)
(e)
(f)
(g)
Bal.

Problem 2-11A

Problem 2-12A

Exercise 2-1B

Account	Classification
Cash	_____
Accounts Payable	_____
Supplies	_____
Bill Jones, Drawing	_____
Prepaid Insurance	_____
Accounts Receivable	_____
Bill Jones, Capital	_____

Exercise 2-2B

Assets	=	Liabilities	+	Owner's Equity
_____	=	$20,000	+	$ 5,000
$30,000	=	$15,000	+	_____
$20,000	=	_____	+	$10,000

Exercise 2-3B

	Assets	=	Liabilities	+	Owner's Equity
(a)	_____		_____		_____
Bal.	_____		_____		_____
(b)	_____		_____		_____
Bal.	_____		_____		_____
(c)	_____		_____		_____
	_____		_____		_____
Bal.	_____		_____		_____
(d)	_____		_____		_____
Bal.	_____		_____		_____

Exercise 2-4B

Assets	=	Liabilities	+	Capital	–	Drawing	+	Revenues	–	Expenses	Description
						Owner's Equity					

Bal.
from
E 2-3B

(d)

(e)

(f)

(g)

(h)

(i)

(j)

(k)

Bal.

Exercise 2-5B

Account	Classification	Financial Statement
Cash	_____	_____
Rent Expense	_____	_____
Accounts Payable	_____	_____
Service Fees	_____	_____
Supplies	_____	_____
Wages Expense	_____	_____
Amanda Wong, Drawing	_____	_____
Amanda Wong, Capital	_____	_____
Prepaid Insurance	_____	_____
Accounts Receivable	_____	_____

Exercise 2-6B

Exercise 2-7B

Problem 2-8B

	Assets	=	Liabilities	+	Owner's Equity
1.	_____		_____		_____
2.	_____		_____		_____
3.	_____		_____		_____

Problem 2-9B: See page WP-13

Problem 2-10B

Problem 2-9B

	Assets			=	Liabilities	+	Owner's Equity				
	(Items Owned)				(Amts. Owed)		(Owner's Investment)		(Earnings)		
	Accounts	Office	Prepaid		Accounts		D. Segal,	D. Segal,			Description
Cash	+ Receivable	+ Supplies	+ Insurance	=	Payable	+	Capital −	Drawing	+ Revenues −	Expenses	
(a)											
(b)											
(c)											
(d)											
(e)											
(f)											
(g)											
Bal.											

Problem 2-11B

Problem 2-12B

Mastery Problem

1.

	Assets						=	Liabilities (Amts. Owed)	+	Owner's Equity				
		(Items Owned)								(Owner's Investment)		(Earnings)		
Cash	+ Accts. Rec.	+ Sup-plies	+ Prepaid Ins.	+ Tools	+ Van	=	Accts. Payable	+	L. Vozniak, Capital	− L. Vozniak, Drawing	+	Rev.	− Exp.	Description
(a)														
(b)														
(c)														
(d)														
(e)														
(f)														
(g)														
(h)														
(i)														
(j)														
(k)														
(l)														
(m)														
(n)														
(o)														
(p)														

2. Bal.

Mastery Problem (Continued)

3.

4.

Mastery Problem (Concluded)

5.

Challenge Problem

Cash from customers			
Cash paid for wages			
Cash paid for rent			
Cash paid for utilities			
Cash paid for insurance			
Cash paid for supplies			
Cash paid for phone			
Total cash paid for operating items			
Difference between cash received from customers and			
cash paid for goods and services			

Exercise 3-1A

	Cash	
500		100
400		200
600		

Exercise 3-2A

a. The cash account is increased with a .... _____

b. The owner's capital account is increased with a .... _____

c. The delivery equipment account is increased with a .... _____

d. The cash account is decreased with a .... _____

e. The liability account Accounts Payable is increased with a .... _____

f. The revenue account Delivery Fees is increased with a .... _____

g. The asset account Accounts Receivable is increased with a .... _____

h. The rent expense account is increased with a .... _____

i. The owner's drawing account is increased with a .... _____

Exercise 3-3A

1. and 2.

	Cash			Richard Gibbs, Capital	

	Supplies			Utilities Expense	

Exercise 3-4A

<u>Account</u>	<u>Debit or Credit</u>
1. Cash	_____
2. Wages Expense	_____
3. Accounts Payable	_____
4. Owner's Drawing	_____
5. Supplies	_____
6. Owner's Capital	_____
7. Equipment	_____

Exercises 3-5A and 3-6A: See page WP-21

Exercises 3-5A and 3-6A

Assets		=	Liabilities		+	Owner's Equity		
Dr. +	Cr. −		Dr. −	Cr. +		Dr. −	Cr. +	

Drawing		Expenses		Revenues	
Dr. +	Cr. −	Dr. +	Cr. −	Dr. −	Cr. +

Exercise 3-7A

Assets		=	Liabilities		+	Owner's Equity	
Dr.	Cr.		Dr.	Cr.		Dr.	Cr.
+	−		−	+		−	+

Drawing

Dr.	Cr.
+	−

Expenses

Dr.	Cr.
+	−

Revenues

Dr.	Cr.
−	+

Exercise 3-8A

ACCOUNT	DEBIT BALANCE	CREDIT BALANCE

Exercise 3-9A

ACCOUNT	DEBIT BALANCE	CREDIT BALANCE

Exercise 3-10A

Exercise 3-11A

Exercise 3-12A

Problem 3-13A
1. and 2.

Assets		=	Liabilities		+	Owner's Equity	
Dr. +	Cr. −		Dr. −	Cr. +		Dr. −	Cr. +

Drawing
| Dr. + | Cr. − |

Expenses
| Dr. + | Cr. − |

Revenues
| Dr. − | Cr. + |

Problem 3-13A (Concluded)

3.

ACCOUNT	DEBIT BALANCE	CREDIT BALANCE

Problem 3-14A

1.

    a. Total revenue for the month.. _____

    b. Total expenses for the month .... _____

    c. Net income for the month.. _____

2.

    a. Wilhelm Kohl's original investment in the business ....

        _____

        + Net income for the month..................................... _____

        − Owner's drawing .... _____

        Increase in capital .... _____

        = Ending owner's equity.. _____

    b. End-of-month accounting equation:

Assets	=	Liabilities	+	Owner's Equity
_____		_____		_____

Problem 3-15A

1.

Problem 3-15A (Concluded)

2.

3.

Exercise 3-1B

Accounts Payable	
300	450
250	350
	150

Exercise 3-2B

a.   The asset account Prepaid Insurance is increased with a.................................   _____

b.   The owner's drawing account is increased with a...   _____

c.   The asset account Accounts Receivable is decreased with a ....   _____

d.   The liability account Accounts Payable is decreased with a.............................   _____

e.   The owner's capital account is increased with a..   _____

f.   The revenue account Professional Fees is increased with a............................   _____

g.   The expense account Repair Expense is increased with a ....   _____

h.   The asset account Cash is decreased with a ....   _____

i.   The asset account Delivery Equipment is decreased with a.............................   _____

Exercise 3-3B

1. and 2.

Cash			Roberto Alvarez, Capital	

Supplies			Utilities Expense	

Exercise 3-4B

	Account	Debit or Credit
1.	Cash	_____
2.	Rent Expense	_____
3.	Notes Payable	_____
4.	Owner's Drawing	_____
5.	Accounts Receivable	_____
6.	Owner's Capital	_____
7.	Tools	_____

Exercises 3-5B and 3-6B: See page WP-32

Exercises 3-5B and 3-6B

Assets			=	Liabilities			+	Owner's Equity		
Dr.		Cr.		Dr.		Cr.		Dr.		Cr.
+		–		–		+		–		+

Drawing
Dr.		Cr.
+		–

Expenses
Dr.		Cr.
+		–

Revenues
Dr.		Cr.
–		+

Exercise 3-7B

Assets			=	Liabilities			+	Owner's Equity		
Dr. +	Cr. –			Dr. –	Cr. +			Dr. –	Cr. +	

Drawing			Expenses			Revenues		
Dr. +	Cr. –		Dr. +	Cr. –		Dr. –	Cr. +	

Exercise 3-8B

ACCOUNT	DEBIT BALANCE	CREDIT BALANCE

Exercise 3-9B

ACCOUNT	DEBIT BALANCE	CREDIT BALANCE

Exercise 3-10B

Exercise 3-11B

Exercise 3-12B

Problem 3-13B
1. and 2.

Assets			=	Liabilities			+	Owner's Equity		
Dr.		Cr.		Dr.		Cr.		Dr.		Cr.
+		–		–		+		–		+

Owner's Equity accounts:

Drawing			Expenses			Revenues		
Dr.		Cr.	Dr.		Cr.	Dr.		Cr.
+		–	+		–	–		+

Problem 3-13B (Concluded)

3.

ACCOUNT	DEBIT BALANCE	CREDIT BALANCE

Problem 3-14B

1.

    a. Total revenue for the month .... _____

    b. Total expenses for the month.. _____

    c. Net income for the month .... _____

2.

    a. Sue Jantz's original investment in the business .... _____

         + Net income for the month .... _____

         – Owner's drawing... _____

         Increase in capital... _____

         = Ending owner's equity .... _____

    b. End-of-month accounting equation:

Assets	=	Liabilities	+	Owner's Equity
_____		_____		_____

Problem 3-15B

1.

Problem 3-15B (Concluded)

2.

3.

Mastery Problem

1. and 2.

	Assets		=		Liabilities		+		Owner's Equity	
Dr. +		Cr. –		Dr. –		Cr. +		Dr. –		Cr. +

Drawing
| Dr. + | Cr. – |

Expenses
| Dr. + | Cr. – |

Revenues
| Dr. – | Cr. + |

Mastery Problem (Continued)

3.

ACCOUNT	DEBIT BALANCE	CREDIT BALANCE

4.

Mastery Problem (Concluded)

5.

6.

Challenge Problem

1.

2.

Exercise 4-1A

1. _____ Check stubs or check register

2. _____ Purchase invoice from suppliers (vendors)

3. _____ Sales tickets or invoices to customers

4. _____ Receipts or cash register tapes

a. A good or service has been sold.

b. Cash has been received by the business.

c. Cash has been paid by the business.

d. Goods or services have been purchased by the business.

Exercise 4-2A

Transaction	Debit	Credit
1. Invested cash in the business, $5,000.	_____	_____
2. Paid office rent, $500.	_____	_____
3. Purchased office supplies on account, $300.	_____	_____
4. Received cash for services rendered (fees), $400.	_____	_____
5. Paid cash on account, $50.	_____	_____
6. Rendered services on account, $300.	_____	_____
7. Received cash for an amount owed by a customer, $100.	_____	_____

Exercise 4-3A

Exercise 4-3A (Concluded)

	Total Debits: Total Credits:

Exercise 4-4A

GENERAL JOURNAL   PAGE 1

	DATE	DESCRIPTION	POST. REF.	DEBIT	CREDIT	
1						1
2						2
3						3
4						4
5						5
6						6
7						7
8						8
9						9
10						10
11						11
12						12
13						13
14						14
15						15
16						16
17						17
18						18
19						19
20						20
21						21
22						22
23						23
24						24

Exercise 4-4A (Concluded)

GENERAL JOURNAL

	DATE		DESCRIPTION	POST. REF.	DEBIT	CREDIT	
1							1
2							2
3							3
4							4
5							5
6							6
7							7
8							8
9							9
10							10
11							11
12							12
13							13
14							14
15							15
16							16
17							17
18							18
19							19
20							20
21							21
22							22
23							23
24							24
25							25
26							26
27							27
28							28
29							29
30							30
31							31
32							32
33							33
34							34
35							35
36							36

Exercise 4-5A

GENERAL LEDGER

ACCOUNT _____ ACCOUNT NO. _____

DATE		ITEM	POST. REF.	DEBIT	CREDIT	BALANCE	
						DEBIT	CREDIT

ACCOUNT _____ ACCOUNT NO. _____

DATE		ITEM	POST. REF.	DEBIT	CREDIT	BALANCE	
						DEBIT	CREDIT

ACCOUNT _____ ACCOUNT NO. _____

DATE		ITEM	POST. REF.	DEBIT	CREDIT	BALANCE	
						DEBIT	CREDIT

Exercise 4-5A (Continued)

ACCOUNT _____ ACCOUNT NO. _____

DATE	ITEM	POST. REF.	DEBIT	CREDIT	BALANCE DEBIT	CREDIT

ACCOUNT _____ ACCOUNT NO. _____

DATE	ITEM	POST. REF.	DEBIT	CREDIT	BALANCE DEBIT	CREDIT

ACCOUNT _____ ACCOUNT NO. _____

DATE	ITEM	POST. REF.	DEBIT	CREDIT	BALANCE DEBIT	CREDIT

ACCOUNT _____ ACCOUNT NO. _____

DATE	ITEM	POST. REF.	DEBIT	CREDIT	BALANCE DEBIT	CREDIT

Exercise 4-5A (Continued)

ACCOUNT   ACCOUNT NO.

DATE	ITEM	POST. REF.	DEBIT	CREDIT	BALANCE	
					DEBIT	CREDIT

ACCOUNT   ACCOUNT NO.

DATE	ITEM	POST. REF.	DEBIT	CREDIT	BALANCE	
					DEBIT	CREDIT

ACCOUNT   ACCOUNT NO.

DATE	ITEM	POST. REF.	DEBIT	CREDIT	BALANCE	
					DEBIT	CREDIT

ACCOUNT   ACCOUNT NO.

DATE	ITEM	POST. REF.	DEBIT	CREDIT	BALANCE	
					DEBIT	CREDIT

ACCOUNT   ACCOUNT NO.

DATE	ITEM	POST. REF.	DEBIT	CREDIT	BALANCE	
					DEBIT	CREDIT

Exercise 4-5A (Concluded)

ACCOUNT TITLE	ACCT. NO.	DEBIT BALANCE	CREDIT BALANCE

Exercise 4-6A

Exercise 4-6A (Concluded)

Exercise 4-7A

Exercise 4-7A (Concluded)

Exercise 4-8A

GENERAL JOURNAL   PAGE

	DATE		DESCRIPTION	POST. REF.	DEBIT	CREDIT	
15	May	17	Office Equipment		4 0 0 00		15
16			Cash			4 0 0 00	16
17			Purchased copy paper				17
18							18
23		23	Cash	101	1 0 0 0 00		23
24			Service Fees	401		1 0 0 0 00	24
25			Received cash for services previously earned				25
26							26
27							27
28							28
29							29
30							30
31							31
32							32
33							33

Problem 4-9A
2. (For 1. and 3., see page WP-58.)

GENERAL JOURNAL

	DATE		DESCRIPTION	POST. REF.	DEBIT	CREDIT	
1							1
2							2
3							3
4							4
5							5
6							6
7							7
8							8
9							9
10							10
11							11
12							12
13							13
14							14
15							15
16							16
17							17
18							18
19							19
20							20
21							21
22							22
23							23
24							24
25							25
26							26
27							27
28							28
29							29
30							30
31							31
32							32
33							33
34							34
35							35
36							36

Problem 4-9A (Continued)

GENERAL JOURNAL

	DATE	DESCRIPTION	POST. REF.	DEBIT	CREDIT	
1						1
2						2
3						3
4						4
5						5
6						6
7						7
8						8
9						9
10						10
11						11
12						12
13						13
14						14
15						15
16						16
17						17
18						18
19						19
20						20
21						21
22						22
23						23
24						24
25						25
26						26
27						27
28						28
29						29
30						30
31						31
32						32
33						33
34						34
35						35
36						36

Problem 4-9A (Continued)

GENERAL JOURNAL

	DATE	DESCRIPTION	POST. REF.	DEBIT	CREDIT	
1						1
2						2
3						3
4						4
5						5
6						6
7						7
8						8
9						9
10						10
11						11
12						12
13						13
14						14
15						15
16						16
17						17
18						18
19						19
20						20
21						21
22						22
23						23
24						24
25						25
26						26
27						27
28						28
29						29
30						30
31						31
32						32
33						33
34						34
35						35
36						36

Problem 4-9A (Continued)

1. and 3.

GENERAL LEDGER

ACCOUNT Cash   ACCOUNT NO. 101

DATE	ITEM	POST. REF.	DEBIT	CREDIT	BALANCE	
					DEBIT	CREDIT

ACCOUNT Office Supplies   ACCOUNT NO. 142

DATE	ITEM	POST. REF.	DEBIT	CREDIT	BALANCE	
					DEBIT	CREDIT

Problem 4-9A (Continued)

ACCOUNT Office Equipment   ACCOUNT NO. 181

DATE	ITEM	POST. REF.	DEBIT	CREDIT	BALANCE DEBIT	CREDIT

ACCOUNT Accounts Payable   ACCOUNT NO. 202

DATE	ITEM	POST. REF.	DEBIT	CREDIT	BALANCE DEBIT	CREDIT

ACCOUNT Annette Creighton, Capital   ACCOUNT NO. 311

DATE	ITEM	POST. REF.	DEBIT	CREDIT	BALANCE DEBIT	CREDIT

ACCOUNT Annette Creighton, Drawing   ACCOUNT NO. 312

DATE	ITEM	POST. REF.	DEBIT	CREDIT	BALANCE DEBIT	CREDIT

Problem 4-9A (Continued)

ACCOUNT Consulting Fees   ACCOUNT NO. 401

DATE	ITEM	POST. REF.	DEBIT	CREDIT	BALANCE DEBIT	CREDIT

ACCOUNT Wages Expense   ACCOUNT NO. 511

DATE	ITEM	POST. REF.	DEBIT	CREDIT	BALANCE DEBIT	CREDIT

ACCOUNT Advertising Expense   ACCOUNT NO. 512

DATE	ITEM	POST. REF.	DEBIT	CREDIT	BALANCE DEBIT	CREDIT

ACCOUNT Rent Expense   ACCOUNT NO. 521

DATE	ITEM	POST. REF.	DEBIT	CREDIT	BALANCE DEBIT	CREDIT

Problem 4-9A (Continued)

ACCOUNT Phone Expense   ACCOUNT NO. 525

DATE	ITEM	POST. REF.	DEBIT	CREDIT	BALANCE DEBIT	BALANCE CREDIT

ACCOUNT Transportation Expense   ACCOUNT NO. 526

DATE	ITEM	POST. REF.	DEBIT	CREDIT	BALANCE DEBIT	BALANCE CREDIT

ACCOUNT Utilities Expense   ACCOUNT NO. 533

DATE	ITEM	POST. REF.	DEBIT	CREDIT	BALANCE DEBIT	BALANCE CREDIT

ACCOUNT Miscellaneous Expense   ACCOUNT NO. 549

DATE	ITEM	POST. REF.	DEBIT	CREDIT	BALANCE DEBIT	BALANCE CREDIT

Problem 4-9A (Continued)

4.

ACCOUNT TITLE	ACCT. NO.	DEBIT BALANCE	CREDIT BALANCE

Problem 4-9A (Continued)

5.

Problem 4-9A (Concluded)

Problem 4-10A
2. (For 1. and 3., see page WP-68.)

GENERAL JOURNAL

PAGE 7

	DATE		DESCRIPTION	POST. REF.	DEBIT	CREDIT	
1							1
2							2
3							3
4							4
5							5
6							6
7							7
8							8
9							9
10							10
11							11
12							12
13							13
14							14
15							15
16							16
17							17
18							18
19							19
20							20
21							21
22							22
23							23
24							24
25							25
26							26
27							27
28							28
29							29
30							30
31							31
32							32
33							33
34							34

Problem 4-10A (Continued)

GENERAL JOURNAL

	DATE		DESCRIPTION	POST. REF.	DEBIT	CREDIT	
1							1
2							2
3							3
4							4
5							5
6							6
7							7
8							8
9							9
10							10
11							11
12							12
13							13
14							14
15							15
16							16
17							17
18							18
19							19
20							20
21							21
22							22
23							23
24							24
25							25
26							26
27							27
28							28
29							29
30							30
31							31
32							32
33							33
34							34
35							35
36							36

Problem 4-10A (Continued)

GENERAL JOURNAL

	DATE		DESCRIPTION	POST. REF.	DEBIT	CREDIT	
1							1
2							2
3							3
4							4
5							5
6							6
7							7
8							8
9							9
10							10
11							11
12							12
13							13
14							14
15							15
16							16
17							17
18							18
19							19
20							20
21							21
22							22
23							23
24							24
25							25
26							26
27							27
28							28
29							29
30							30
31							31
32							32
33							33
34							34
35							35
36							36

Problem 4-10A (Continued)

1. and 3.

ACCOUNT Cash

GENERAL LEDGER

ACCOUNT NO. 101

DATE	ITEM	POST. REF.	DEBIT	CREDIT	BALANCE DEBIT	BALANCE CREDIT

Problem 4-10A (Continued)

ACCOUNT Accounts Receivable   ACCOUNT NO. 122

DATE	ITEM	POST. REF.	DEBIT	CREDIT	BALANCE DEBIT	BALANCE CREDIT

ACCOUNT Office Supplies   ACCOUNT NO. 142

DATE	ITEM	POST. REF.	DEBIT	CREDIT	BALANCE DEBIT	BALANCE CREDIT

ACCOUNT Office Equipment   ACCOUNT NO. 181

DATE	ITEM	POST. REF.	DEBIT	CREDIT	BALANCE DEBIT	BALANCE CREDIT

ACCOUNT Delivery Truck   ACCOUNT NO. 185

DATE	ITEM	POST. REF.	DEBIT	CREDIT	BALANCE DEBIT	BALANCE CREDIT

Problem 4-10A (Continued)

ACCOUNT Accounts Payable   ACCOUNT NO. 202

DATE	ITEM	POST. REF.	DEBIT	CREDIT	BALANCE DEBIT	BALANCE CREDIT

ACCOUNT Jim Andrews, Capital   ACCOUNT NO. 311

DATE	ITEM	POST. REF.	DEBIT	CREDIT	BALANCE DEBIT	BALANCE CREDIT

ACCOUNT Jim Andrews, Drawing   ACCOUNT NO. 312

DATE	ITEM	POST. REF.	DEBIT	CREDIT	BALANCE DEBIT	BALANCE CREDIT

ACCOUNT Delivery Fees   ACCOUNT NO. 401

DATE	ITEM	POST. REF.	DEBIT	CREDIT	BALANCE DEBIT	BALANCE CREDIT

Problem 4-10A (Continued)

ACCOUNT Wages Expense   ACCOUNT NO. 511

DATE		ITEM	POST. REF.	DEBIT	CREDIT	BALANCE	
						DEBIT	CREDIT

ACCOUNT Advertising Expense   ACCOUNT NO. 512

DATE		ITEM	POST. REF.	DEBIT	CREDIT	BALANCE	
						DEBIT	CREDIT

ACCOUNT Rent Expense   ACCOUNT NO. 521

DATE		ITEM	POST. REF.	DEBIT	CREDIT	BALANCE	
						DEBIT	CREDIT

ACCOUNT Phone Expense   ACCOUNT NO. 525

DATE		ITEM	POST. REF.	DEBIT	CREDIT	BALANCE	
						DEBIT	CREDIT

Problem 4-10A (Continued)

ACCOUNT Electricity Expense   ACCOUNT NO. 533

DATE	ITEM	POST. REF.	DEBIT	CREDIT	BALANCE DEBIT	BALANCE CREDIT

ACCOUNT Charitable Contributions Expense   ACCOUNT NO. 534

DATE	ITEM	POST. REF.	DEBIT	CREDIT	BALANCE DEBIT	BALANCE CREDIT

ACCOUNT Gas and Oil Expense   ACCOUNT NO. 538

DATE	ITEM	POST. REF.	DEBIT	CREDIT	BALANCE DEBIT	BALANCE CREDIT

ACCOUNT Miscellaneous Expense   ACCOUNT NO. 549

DATE	ITEM	POST. REF.	DEBIT	CREDIT	BALANCE DEBIT	BALANCE CREDIT

Problem 4-10A (Concluded)

4.

ACCOUNT TITLE	ACCT. NO.	DEBIT BALANCE	CREDIT BALANCE

Problem 4-11A

GENERAL JOURNAL

PAGE

	DATE	DESCRIPTION	POST. REF.	DEBIT	CREDIT	
1						1
2						2
3						3
4						4
5						5
6						6
7						7
8						8
9						9
10						10
11						11
12						12
13						13
14						14
15						15
16						16
17						17
18						18
19						19
20						20

Exercise 4-1B

1. Cash register tape

_____

_____

2. Sales ticket (issued to customer)

_____

_____

3. Purchase invoice (received from supplier or vendor)

_____

_____

4. Check stub

_____

_____

Exercise 4-2B

Transaction	Debit	Credit
1. Invested cash in the business, $1,000.	_____	_____
2. Performed services on account, $200.	_____	_____
3. Purchased office equipment on account, $500.	_____	_____
4. Received cash on account for services previously rendered, $200.	_____	_____
5. Made a payment on account, $100.	_____	_____

Exercise 4-3B

Total Debits: _____ Total Credits: _____

Exercise 4-4B

GENERAL JOURNAL

	DATE		DESCRIPTION	POST. REF.	DEBIT	CREDIT	
1							1
2							2
3							3
4							4
5							5
6							6
7							7
8							8
9							9
10							10
11							11
12							12
13							13
14							14
15							15
16							16
17							17
18							18
19							19
20							20
21							21
22							22
23							23
24							24
25							25
26							26
27							27
28							28
29							29
30							30
31							31
32							32
33							33
34							34
35							35
36							36

Exercise 4-4B (Concluded)

GENERAL JOURNAL

PAGE   2

	DATE		DESCRIPTION	POST. REF.	DEBIT	CREDIT	
1							1
2							2
3							3
4							4
5							5
6							6
7							7
8							8
9							9
10							10
11							11
12							12
13							13
14							14
15							15
16							16
17							17
18							18
19							19
20							20
21							21
22							22
23							23
24							24
25							25
26							26
27							27
28							28
29							29
30							30
31							31
32							32
33							33
34							34
35							35
36							36

Exercise 4-5B

GENERAL LEDGER

ACCOUNT _____   ACCOUNT NO. _____

DATE	ITEM	POST. REF.	DEBIT	CREDIT	BALANCE	
					DEBIT	CREDIT

ACCOUNT _____   ACCOUNT NO. _____

DATE	ITEM	POST. REF.	DEBIT	CREDIT	BALANCE	
					DEBIT	CREDIT

ACCOUNT _____   ACCOUNT NO. _____

DATE	ITEM	POST. REF.	DEBIT	CREDIT	BALANCE	
					DEBIT	CREDIT

Exercise 4-5B (Continued)

ACCOUNT _____   ACCOUNT NO. _____

DATE	ITEM	POST. REF.	DEBIT	CREDIT	BALANCE DEBIT	BALANCE CREDIT

ACCOUNT _____   ACCOUNT NO. _____

DATE	ITEM	POST. REF.	DEBIT	CREDIT	BALANCE DEBIT	BALANCE CREDIT

ACCOUNT _____   ACCOUNT NO. _____

DATE	ITEM	POST. REF.	DEBIT	CREDIT	BALANCE DEBIT	BALANCE CREDIT

ACCOUNT _____   ACCOUNT NO. _____

DATE	ITEM	POST. REF.	DEBIT	CREDIT	BALANCE DEBIT	BALANCE CREDIT

Exercise 4-5B (Continued)

ACCOUNT _____ ACCOUNT NO. _____

DATE	ITEM	POST. REF.	DEBIT	CREDIT	BALANCE	
					DEBIT	CREDIT

ACCOUNT _____ ACCOUNT NO. _____

DATE	ITEM	POST. REF.	DEBIT	CREDIT	BALANCE	
					DEBIT	CREDIT

ACCOUNT _____ ACCOUNT NO. _____

DATE	ITEM	POST. REF.	DEBIT	CREDIT	BALANCE	
					DEBIT	CREDIT

ACCOUNT _____ ACCOUNT NO. _____

DATE	ITEM	POST. REF.	DEBIT	CREDIT	BALANCE	
					DEBIT	CREDIT

ACCOUNT _____ ACCOUNT NO. _____

DATE	ITEM	POST. REF.	DEBIT	CREDIT	BALANCE	
					DEBIT	CREDIT

Exercise 4-5B (Concluded)

ACCOUNT TITLE	ACCT. NO.	DEBIT BALANCE	CREDIT BALANCE

Exercise 4-6B

Exercise 4-6B (Concluded)

<table>
<tr><td></td><td></td><td></td></tr>
<tr><td></td><td></td><td></td></tr>
<tr><td></td><td></td><td></td></tr>
<tr><td></td><td></td><td></td></tr>
<tr><td></td><td></td><td></td></tr>
<tr><td></td><td></td><td></td></tr>
<tr><td></td><td></td><td></td></tr>
<tr><td></td><td></td><td></td></tr>
<tr><td></td><td></td><td></td></tr>
<tr><td></td><td></td><td></td></tr>
<tr><td></td><td></td><td></td></tr>
</table>

<table>
<tr><td></td><td></td><td></td><td></td></tr>
<tr><td></td><td></td><td></td><td></td></tr>
<tr><td></td><td></td><td></td><td></td></tr>
<tr><td></td><td></td><td></td><td></td></tr>
<tr><td></td><td></td><td></td><td></td></tr>
<tr><td></td><td></td><td></td><td></td></tr>
<tr><td></td><td></td><td></td><td></td></tr>
<tr><td></td><td></td><td></td><td></td></tr>
<tr><td></td><td></td><td></td><td></td></tr>
<tr><td></td><td></td><td></td><td></td></tr>
<tr><td></td><td></td><td></td><td></td></tr>
<tr><td></td><td></td><td></td><td></td></tr>
</table>

Exercise 4-7B

Exercise 4-7B (Concluded)

Exercise 4-8B

GENERAL JOURNAL

PAGE

	DATE		DESCRIPTION	POST. REF.	DEBIT	CREDIT	
15	Apr.	6	Office Supplies		5 3 0 00		15
16			Cash			5 3 0 00	16
17			Purchased office equipment				17
18							18
23		21	Cash	101	3 0 0 00		23
24			Service Fees	401		3 0 0 00	24
25			Revenue earned from services				25
26			previously rendered				26
27							27
28							28
29							29
30							30
31							31
32							32
33							33

Problem 4-9B

2. (For 1. and 3., see page WP-88.)

GENERAL JOURNAL

	DATE		DESCRIPTION	POST. REF.	DEBIT	CREDIT	
1							1
2							2
3							3
4							4
5							5
6							6
7							7
8							8
9							9
10							10
11							11
12							12
13							13
14							14
15							15
16							16
17							17
18							18
19							19
20							20
21							21
22							22
23							23
24							24
25							25
26							26
27							27
28							28
29							29
30							30
31							31
32							32
33							33
34							34
35							35
36							36

Problem 4-9B (Continued)

GENERAL JOURNAL

	DATE		DESCRIPTION	POST. REF.	DEBIT	CREDIT	
1							1
2							2
3							3
4							4
5							5
6							6
7							7
8							8
9							9
10							10
11							11
12							12
13							13
14							14
15							15
16							16
17							17
18							18
19							19
20							20
21							21
22							22
23							23
24							24
25							25
26							26
27							27
28							28
29							29
30							30
31							31
32							32
33							33
34							34
35							35
36							36

Problem 4-9B (Continued)

GENERAL JOURNAL   PAGE 3

	DATE		DESCRIPTION	POST. REF.	DEBIT	CREDIT	
1							1
2							2
3							3
4							4
5							5
6							6
7							7
8							8
9							9
10							10
11							11
12							12
13							13
14							14
15							15
16							16
17							17
18							18
19							19
20							20
21							21
22							22
23							23
24							24
25							25
26							26
27							27
28							28
29							29
30							30
31							31
32							32
33							33
34							34
35							35
36							36

Problem 4-9B (Continued)

1. and 3.

GENERAL LEDGER

ACCOUNT Cash   ACCOUNT NO. 101

DATE	ITEM	POST. REF.	DEBIT	CREDIT	BALANCE DEBIT	BALANCE CREDIT

ACCOUNT Accounts Receivable   ACCOUNT NO. 122

DATE	ITEM	POST. REF.	DEBIT	CREDIT	BALANCE DEBIT	BALANCE CREDIT

Problem 4-9B (Continued)

ACCOUNT Office Supplies

ACCOUNT NO. 142

DATE		ITEM	POST. REF.	DEBIT	CREDIT	BALANCE	
						DEBIT	CREDIT

ACCOUNT Office Equipment

ACCOUNT NO. 181

DATE		ITEM	POST. REF.	DEBIT	CREDIT	BALANCE	
						DEBIT	CREDIT

ACCOUNT Accounts Payable

ACCOUNT NO. 202

DATE		ITEM	POST. REF.	DEBIT	CREDIT	BALANCE	
						DEBIT	CREDIT

ACCOUNT Benito Mendez, Capital

ACCOUNT NO. 311

DATE		ITEM	POST. REF.	DEBIT	CREDIT	BALANCE	
						DEBIT	CREDIT

Problem 4-9B (Continued)

ACCOUNT Benito Mendez, Drawing   ACCOUNT NO. 312

DATE	ITEM	POST. REF.	DEBIT	CREDIT	BALANCE	
					DEBIT	CREDIT

ACCOUNT Appraisal Fees   ACCOUNT NO. 401

DATE	ITEM	POST. REF.	DEBIT	CREDIT	BALANCE	
					DEBIT	CREDIT

ACCOUNT Wages Expense   ACCOUNT NO. 511

DATE	ITEM	POST. REF.	DEBIT	CREDIT	BALANCE	
					DEBIT	CREDIT

ACCOUNT Advertising Expense   ACCOUNT NO. 512

DATE	ITEM	POST. REF.	DEBIT	CREDIT	BALANCE	
					DEBIT	CREDIT

Problem 4-9B (Continued)

ACCOUNT Rent Expense   ACCOUNT NO. 521

DATE	ITEM	POST. REF.	DEBIT	CREDIT	BALANCE	
					DEBIT	CREDIT

ACCOUNT Phone Expense   ACCOUNT NO. 525

DATE	ITEM	POST. REF.	DEBIT	CREDIT	BALANCE	
					DEBIT	CREDIT

ACCOUNT Transportation Expense   ACCOUNT NO 526

DATE	ITEM	POST. REF.	DEBIT	CREDIT	BALANCE	
					DEBIT	CREDIT

ACCOUNT Electricity Expense   ACCOUNT NO. 533

DATE	ITEM	POST. REF.	DEBIT	CREDIT	BALANCE	
					DEBIT	CREDIT

ACCOUNT Miscellaneous Expense   ACCOUNT NO. 549

DATE	ITEM	POST. REF.	DEBIT	CREDIT	BALANCE	
					DEBIT	CREDIT

Problem 4-9B (Continued)

4.

ACCOUNT TITLE	ACCT. NO.	DEBIT BALANCE	CREDIT BALANCE

Problem 4-9B (Continued)

5.

_____

_____

_____

_____

_____

Problem 4-9B (Concluded)

Problem 4-10B

2. (For 1. and 3., see page WP-98.)

(For 1. and 3., see page WP-98.)

GENERAL JOURNAL   PAGE 7

	DATE	DESCRIPTION	POST. REF.	DEBIT	CREDIT	
1						1
2						2
3						3
4						4
5						5
6						6
7						7
8						8
9						9
10						10
11						11
12						12
13						13
14						14
15						15
16						16
17						17
18						18
19						19
20						20
21						21
22						22
23						23
24						24
25						25
26						26
27						27
28						28
29						29
30						30
31						31
32						32
33						33
34						34

Problem 4-10B (Continued)

GENERAL JOURNAL

	DATE		DESCRIPTION	POST. REF.	DEBIT	CREDIT	
1							1
2							2
3							3
4							4
5							5
6							6
7							7
8							8
9							9
10							10
11							11
12							12
13							13
14							14
15							15
16							16
17							17
18							18
19							19
20							20
21							21
22							22
23							23
24							24
25							25
26							26
27							27
28							28
29							29
30							30
31							31
32							32
33							33
34							34
35							35
36							36

Problem 4-10B (Continued)

GENERAL JOURNAL

	DATE		DESCRIPTION	POST. REF.	DEBIT	CREDIT	
1							1
2							2
3							3
4							4
5							5
6							6
7							7
8							8
9							9
10							10
11							11
12							12
13							13
14							14
15							15
16							16
17							17
18							18
19							19
20							20
21							21
22							22
23							23
24							24
25							25
26							26
27							27
28							28
29							29
30							30
31							31
32							32
33							33
34							34
35							35
36							36

Problem 4-10B (Continued)

1. and 3.

GENERAL LEDGER

ACCOUNT Cash   ACCOUNT NO. 101

DATE	ITEM	POST. REF.	DEBIT	CREDIT	BALANCE DEBIT	BALANCE CREDIT

ACCOUNT Accounts Receivable   ACCOUNT NO. 122

DATE	ITEM	POST. REF.	DEBIT	CREDIT	BALANCE DEBIT	BALANCE CREDIT

Problem 4-10B (Continued)

ACCOUNT Tailoring Supplies   ACCOUNT NO. 141

DATE	ITEM	POST. REF.	DEBIT	CREDIT	BALANCE DEBIT	BALANCE CREDIT

ACCOUNT Tailoring Equipment   ACCOUNT NO. 183

DATE	ITEM	POST. REF.	DEBIT	CREDIT	BALANCE DEBIT	BALANCE CREDIT

ACCOUNT Accounts Payable   ACCOUNT NO. 202

DATE	ITEM	POST. REF.	DEBIT	CREDIT	BALANCE DEBIT	BALANCE CREDIT

ACCOUNT Ann Taylor, Capital   ACCOUNT NO. 311

DATE	ITEM	POST. REF.	DEBIT	CREDIT	BALANCE DEBIT	BALANCE CREDIT

Problem 4-10B (Continued)

ACCOUNT Ann Taylor, Drawing   ACCOUNT NO. 312

DATE	ITEM	POST. REF.	DEBIT	CREDIT	BALANCE	
					DEBIT	CREDIT

ACCOUNT Tailoring Fees   ACCOUNT NO. 401

DATE	ITEM	POST. REF.	DEBIT	CREDIT	BALANCE	
					DEBIT	CREDIT

ACCOUNT Wages Expense   ACCOUNT NO. 511

DATE	ITEM	POST. REF.	DEBIT	CREDIT	BALANCE	
					DEBIT	CREDIT

ACCOUNT Advertising Expense   ACCOUNT NO. 512

DATE	ITEM	POST. REF.	DEBIT	CREDIT	BALANCE	
					DEBIT	CREDIT

Problem 4-10B (Continued)

ACCOUNT Rent Expense   ACCOUNT NO. 521

DATE		ITEM	POST. REF.	DEBIT	CREDIT	BALANCE	
						DEBIT	CREDIT

ACCOUNT Phone Expense   ACCOUNT NO. 525

DATE		ITEM	POST. REF.	DEBIT	CREDIT	BALANCE	
						DEBIT	CREDIT

ACCOUNT Electricity Expense   ACCOUNT NO. 533

DATE		ITEM	POST. REF.	DEBIT	CREDIT	BALANCE	
						DEBIT	CREDIT

ACCOUNT Miscellaneous Expense   ACCOUNT NO. 549

DATE		ITEM	POST. REF.	DEBIT	CREDIT	BALANCE	
						DEBIT	CREDIT

Problem 4-10B (Concluded)

4.

ACCOUNT TITLE	ACCT. NO.	DEBIT BALANCE	CREDIT BALANCE

Problem 4-11B

GENERAL JOURNAL   PAGE _____

	DATE		DESCRIPTION	POST. REF.	DEBIT	CREDIT	
1							1
2							2
3							3
4							4
5							5
6							6
7							7
8							8
9							9
10							10
11							11
12							12
13							13
14							14
15							15
16							16
17							17
18							18
19							19
20							20
21							21
22							22
23							23

Mastery Problem
1.

GENERAL JOURNAL

	DATE		DESCRIPTION	POST. REF.	DEBIT	CREDIT	
1							1
2							2
3							3
4							4
5							5
6							6
7							7
8							8
9							9
10							10
11							11
12							12
13							13
14							14
15							15
16							16
17							17
18							18
19							19
20							20
21							21
22							22
23							23
24							24
25							25
26							26
27							27
28							28
29							29
30							30
31							31
32							32
33							33
34							34
35							35

Mastery Problem (Continued)

GENERAL JOURNAL

	DATE	DESCRIPTION	POST. REF.	DEBIT	CREDIT	
1						1
2						2
3						3
4						4
5						5
6						6
7						7
8						8
9						9
10						10
11						11
12						12
13						13
14						14
15						15
16						16
17						17
18						18
19						19
20						20
21						21
22						22
23						23
24						24
25						25
26						26
27						27
28						28
29						29
30						30
31						31
32						32
33						33
34						34
35						35

Mastery Problem (Continued)

GENERAL JOURNAL   PAGE   3

	DATE	DESCRIPTION	POST. REF.	DEBIT	CREDIT	
1						1
2						2
3						3
4						4
5						5
6						6
7						7
8						8
9						9
10						10
11						11
12						12
13						13
14						14
15						15
16						16
17						17
18						18
19						19
20						20
21						21
22						22
23						23
24						24
25						25
26						26
27						27
28						28
29						29
30						30
31						31
32						32
33						33
34						34
35						35

Mastery Problem (Continued)

2.

ACCOUNT Cash   **GENERAL LEDGER**   ACCOUNT NO. 101

DATE	ITEM	POST. REF.	DEBIT	CREDIT	BALANCE	
					DEBIT	CREDIT

ACCOUNT Office Supplies   ACCOUNT NO. 142

DATE	ITEM	POST. REF.	DEBIT	CREDIT	BALANCE	
					DEBIT	CREDIT

ACCOUNT Athletic Equipment   ACCOUNT NO. 183

DATE	ITEM	POST. REF.	DEBIT	CREDIT	BALANCE	
					DEBIT	CREDIT

Mastery Problem (Continued)

ACCOUNT Basketball Facilities   ACCOUNT NO. 184

DATE	ITEM	POST. REF.	DEBIT	CREDIT	BALANCE DEBIT	BALANCE CREDIT

ACCOUNT Accounts Payable   ACCOUNT NO. 202

DATE	ITEM	POST. REF.	DEBIT	CREDIT	BALANCE DEBIT	BALANCE CREDIT

ACCOUNT Barry Bird, Capital   ACCOUNT NO. 311

DATE	ITEM	POST. REF.	DEBIT	CREDIT	BALANCE DEBIT	BALANCE CREDIT

ACCOUNT Barry Bird, Drawing   ACCOUNT NO. 312

DATE	ITEM	POST. REF.	DEBIT	CREDIT	BALANCE DEBIT	BALANCE CREDIT

Mastery Problem (Continued)

ACCOUNT Registration Fees   ACCOUNT NO. 401

DATE	ITEM	POST. REF.	DEBIT	CREDIT	BALANCE	
					DEBIT	CREDIT

ACCOUNT Wages Expense   ACCOUNT NO. 511

DATE	ITEM	POST. REF.	DEBIT	CREDIT	BALANCE	
					DEBIT	CREDIT

ACCOUNT Advertising Expense   ACCOUNT NO. 512

DATE	ITEM	POST. REF.	DEBIT	CREDIT	BALANCE	
					DEBIT	CREDIT

Mastery Problem (Continued)

ACCOUNT Food Expense   ACCOUNT NO.   524

DATE	ITEM	POST. REF.	DEBIT	CREDIT	BALANCE	
					DEBIT	CREDIT

ACCOUNT   Phone Expense   ACCOUNT NO.   525

DATE	ITEM	POST. REF.	DEBIT	CREDIT	BALANCE	
					DEBIT	CREDIT

ACCOUNT   Utilities Expense   ACCOUNT NO.   533

DATE	ITEM	POST. REF.	DEBIT	CREDIT	BALANCE	
					DEBIT	CREDIT

ACCOUNT Postage Expense   ACCOUNT NO.   536

DATE	ITEM	POST. REF.	DEBIT	CREDIT	BALANCE	
					DEBIT	CREDIT

Mastery Problem (Concluded)

3.

_____

_____

_____

ACCOUNT TITLE	ACCT. NO.	DEBIT BALANCE	CREDIT BALANCE

Challenge Problem

1. and 2.

_____

_____

_____

_____

_____

_____

_____

_____

_____

_____

_____

_____

_____

3.

Fred Phaler Consulting

Trial Balance

June 30, 20--

ACCOUNT TITLE	ACCT. NO.	DEBIT BALANCE	CREDIT BALANCE
Cash	101		
Accounts Receivable	122		
Office Supplies	142		
Accounts Payable	202		
Fred Phaler, Capital	311		
Fred Phaler, Drawing	312		
Professional Fees	401		
Wages Expense	511		
Rent Expense	521		
Phone Expense	525		
Automobile Expense	526		
Utilities Expense	533		

Exercise 5-1A

(Balance Sheet) Supplies	(Income Statement) Supplies Expense

GENERAL JOURNAL   PAGE

	DATE	DESCRIPTION	POST. REF.	DEBIT	CREDIT	
1						1
2						2
3						3
4						4
5						5
6						6

Exercise 5-2A

(Balance Sheet) Prepaid Insurance	(Income Statement) Insurance Expense

GENERAL JOURNAL   PAGE

	DATE	DESCRIPTION	POST. REF.	DEBIT	CREDIT	
1						1
2						2
3						3
4						4
5						5
6						6

Exercise 5-3A

(Income Statement) Wages Expense	(Balance Sheet) Wages Payable

GENERAL JOURNAL   PAGE

	DATE	DESCRIPTION	POST. REF.	DEBIT	CREDIT	
1						1
2						2
3						3
4						4

Exercise 5-4A

(Income Statement) Depr. Expense—Delivery Equipment	(Balance Sheet) Accum. Depr.—Delivery Equipment

GENERAL JOURNAL   PAGE

	DATE	DESCRIPTION	POST. REF.	DEBIT	CREDIT	
1						1
2						2
3						3
4						4

Exercise 5-5A

Exercise 5-6A

1.

	(Balance Sheet) Supplies		(Income Statement) Supplies Expense
TB	580		
Bal.	_____		

2.

	(Balance Sheet) Supplies		(Income Statement) Supplies Expense
TB	435		
Bal.	_____		

Exercise 5-7A

1.

	(Balance Sheet) Prepaid Insurance		(Income Statement) Insurance Expense
TB	1,450		
Bal.	_____		

2.

	(Balance Sheet) Prepaid Insurance		(Income Statement) Insurance Expense
TB	1,350		
Bal.	_____		

Exercise 5-8A

GENERAL JOURNAL   PAGE 9

	DATE		DESCRIPTION	POST. REF.	DEBIT	CREDIT	
1			Adjusting Entries				1
2	20-- Dec.	31	Supplies Expense		8 5 00		2
3			Supplies			8 5 00	3
4							4
5		31	Wages Expense		2 2 0 00		5
6			Wages Payable			2 2 0 00	6
7							7
8							8
9							9
10							10
11							11
12							12
13							13
14							14
15							15
16							16
17							17
18							18

Exercise 5-8A (Concluded)

GENERAL LEDGER

ACCOUNT   Supplies   ACCOUNT NO.   141

DATE		ITEM	POST. REF.	DEBIT	CREDIT	BALANCE DEBIT	BALANCE CREDIT
20-- Dec.	1	Balance	✓			1 5 0 00	
	15		J8	5 0 00		2 0 0 00	

ACCOUNT   Wages Payable   ACCOUNT NO.   219

DATE		ITEM	POST. REF.	DEBIT	CREDIT	BALANCE DEBIT	BALANCE CREDIT

ACCOUNT   Wages Expense   ACCOUNT NO.   511

DATE		ITEM	POST. REF.	DEBIT	CREDIT	BALANCE DEBIT	BALANCE CREDIT
20-- Dec.	1	Balance	✓			9 0 0 00	
	15		J8	3 0 0 00		1 2 0 0 00	

ACCOUNT   Supplies Expense   ACCOUNT NO.   523

DATE		ITEM	POST. REF.	DEBIT	CREDIT	BALANCE DEBIT	BALANCE CREDIT

Exercise 5-9A

Jim Jacobs' Furniture Repair
Work Sheet (Partial)
For Year Ended December 31, 20--

	ACCOUNT TITLE	TRIAL BALANCE		ADJUSTMENTS		ADJUSTED TRIAL BALANCE	
		DEBIT	CREDIT	DEBIT	CREDIT	DEBIT	CREDIT
1	Cash	1 0 0 00				1 0 0 00	
2	Supplies	8 5 0 00				2 0 0 00	
3	Prepaid Insurance	9 0 0 00				3 0 0 00	
4	Delivery Equipment	3 6 0 0 00				3 6 0 0 00	
5	Accum. Depr.—Delivery Equip.		6 0 0 00				8 0 0 00
6	Wages Payable						1 0 0 00
7	Jim Jacobs, Capital		4 0 0 0 00				4 0 0 0 00
8	Repair Fees		1 6 5 0 00				1 6 5 0 00
9	Wages Expense	6 0 0 00				7 0 0 00	
10	Advertising Expense	2 0 0 00				2 0 0 00	
11	Supplies Expense					6 5 0 00	
12	Insurance Expense					6 0 0 00	
13	Depr. Exp.—Delivery Equip.					2 0 0 00	
14		6 2 5 0 00	6 2 5 0 00			6 5 5 0 00	6 5 5 0 00
15							
16							
17							
18							
19							
20							
21							
22							
23							
24							
25							

Exercise 5-10A

GENERAL JOURNAL

PAGE ____

	DATE		DESCRIPTION	POST. REF.	DEBIT	CREDIT	
1							1
2							2
3							3
4							4
5							5
6							6
7							7
8							8
9							9
10							10
11							11
12							12
13							13
14							14
15							15

Exercise 5-11A

	Income Statement		Balance Sheet	
	Debit	**Credit**	**Debit**	**Credit**
Cash	_____	_____	_____	_____
Accounts Receivable	_____	_____	_____	_____
Supplies	_____	_____	_____	_____
Prepaid Insurance	_____	_____	_____	_____
Delivery Equipment	_____	_____	_____	_____
Accum. Depr.—Delivery Equip.	_____	_____	_____	_____
Accounts Payable	_____	_____	_____	_____
Wages Payable	_____	_____	_____	_____
Owner, Capital	_____	_____	_____	_____
Owner, Drawing	_____	_____	_____	_____
Delivery Fees	_____	_____	_____	_____
Wages Expense	_____	_____	_____	_____
Rent Expense	_____	_____	_____	_____
Supplies Expense	_____	_____	_____	_____
Insurance Expense	_____	_____	_____	_____
Depr. Exp.—Delivery Equip.	_____	_____	_____	_____

Exercise 5-12A

	Income Statement		Balance Sheet	
	Debit	**Credit**	**Debit**	**Credit**
Net Income	_____	_____	_____	_____
Net Loss	_____	_____	_____	_____

Exercise 5-13A

	Cash Basis	Modified Cash Basis	Accrual Basis
1. Purchase supplies on account.			
2. Make payment on asset previously purchased.			
3. Purchase supplies for cash.			
4. Purchase insurance for cash.			
5. Pay cash for wages.			
6. Pay cash for phone expense.			
7. Pay cash for new equipment.			
8. Wages earned but not paid.			
9. Prepaid item purchased, partly used.			
10. Depreciation on long-term assets.			

Problem 5-14A

Mason's Delivery

Work

For Month Ended

	ACCOUNT TITLE	TRIAL BALANCE						ADJUSTMENTS						
		DEBIT				CREDIT		DEBIT				CREDIT		
1	Cash	1	6	0	0	00								
2	Accounts Receivable		9	4	0	00								
3	Supplies		6	3	5	00								
4	Prepaid Insurance	1	2	0	0	00								
5	Delivery Equipment	6	4	0	0	00								
6	Accum. Depr.—Delivery Equip.													
7	Accounts Payable					1	2	2	0	00				
8	Wages Payable													
9	Jill Mason, Capital					8	0	0	0	00				
10	Jill Mason, Drawing	1	4	0	0	00								
11	Delivery Fees					6	2	0	0	00				
12	Wages Expense	1	5	0	0	00								
13	Advertising Expense		4	6	0	00								
14	Rent Expense		8	0	0	00								
15	Supplies Expense													
16	Phone Expense		1	6	5	00								
17	Insurance Expense													
18	Repair Expense		2	3	0	00								
19	Oil and Gas Expense			9	0	00								
20	Depr. Exp.—Delivery Equip.													
21		15	4	2	0	00	15	4	2	0	00			
22														
23														
24														
25														
26														
27														
28														
29														
30														
31														
32														
33														

Problem 5-14A (Concluded)

Service

Sheet

September 30, 20--

ADJUSTED TRIAL BALANCE		INCOME STATEMENT		BALANCE SHEET		
DEBIT	CREDIT	DEBIT	CREDIT	DEBIT	CREDIT	
						1
						2
						3
						4
						5
						6
						7
						8
						9
						10
						11
						12
						13
						14
						15
						16
						17
						18
						19
						20
						21
						22
						23
						24
						25
						26
						27
						28
						29
						30
						31
						32
						33

Problem 5-15A

Campus Delivery

Work

For Month Ended

	ACCOUNT TITLE	TRIAL BALANCE										ADJUSTMENTS										
		DEBIT					CREDIT					DEBIT					CREDIT					
1	Cash		9	8	0	00																
2	Accounts Receivable		5	9	0	00																
3	Supplies		5	7	5	00																
4	Prepaid Insurance	1	3	0	0	00																
5	Van	5	8	0	0	00																
6	Accumulated Depreciation—Van																					
7	Accounts Payable							9	6	0	00											
8	Wages Payable																					
9	Jason Armstrong, Capital						10	0	0	0	00											
10	Jason Armstrong, Drawing		6	0	0	00																
11	Delivery Fees						2	6	0	0	00											
12	Wages Expense	1	8	0	0	00																
13	Advertising Expense		3	8	0	00																
14	Rent Expense		9	0	0	00																
15	Supplies Expense																					
16	Phone Expense		2	2	0	00																
17	Insurance Expense																					
18	Repair Expense		3	1	5	00																
19	Oil and Gas Expense		1	0	0	00																
20	Depreciation Expense—Van																					
21		13	5	6	0	00	13	5	6	0	00											
22																						
23																						
24																						
25																						
26																						
27																						
28																						
29																						
30																						
31																						
32																						
33																						

Problem 5-15A (Concluded)

Service

Sheet

November 30, 20--

ADJUSTED TRIAL BALANCE		INCOME STATEMENT		BALANCE SHEET		
DEBIT	CREDIT	DEBIT	CREDIT	DEBIT	CREDIT	

(blank worksheet, rows 1–33)

Problem 5-16A

1.

GENERAL JOURNAL

PAGE 5

	DATE		DESCRIPTION	POST. REF.	DEBIT	CREDIT	
1							1
2							2
3							3
4							4
5							5
6							6
7							7
8							8
9							9
10							10
11							11
12							12
13							13
14							14
15							15
16							16
17							17
18							18
19							19
20							20
21							21
22							22
23							23
24							24
25							25
26							26
27							27
28							28
29							29
30							30
31							31
32							32
33							33
34							34
35							35
36							36

Problem 5-16A (Continued)

2.   **GENERAL LEDGER**

ACCOUNT   Supplies   ACCOUNT NO.   141

DATE		ITEM	POST. REF.	DEBIT	CREDIT	BALANCE	
						DEBIT	CREDIT
20-- Nov.	1		J1	4 7 5 00		4 7 5 00	
	15		J4	1 0 0 00		5 7 5 00	

ACCOUNT   Prepaid Insurance   ACCOUNT NO.   145

DATE		ITEM	POST. REF.	DEBIT	CREDIT	BALANCE	
						DEBIT	CREDIT
20-- Nov.	1		J1	1 3 0 0 00		1 3 0 0 00	

ACCOUNT   Accumulated Depreciation—Van   ACCOUNT NO.   185.1

DATE		ITEM	POST. REF.	DEBIT	CREDIT	BALANCE	
						DEBIT	CREDIT

ACCOUNT   Wages Payable   ACCOUNT NO.   219

DATE		ITEM	POST. REF.	DEBIT	CREDIT	BALANCE	
						DEBIT	CREDIT

Problem 5-16A (Concluded)

GENERAL LEDGER

ACCOUNT Wages Expense   ACCOUNT NO. 511

DATE		ITEM	POST. REF.	DEBIT	CREDIT	BALANCE	
						DEBIT	CREDIT
20-- Nov.	15		J3	9 0 0 00		9 0 0 00	
	26		J4	9 0 0 00		1 8 0 0 00	

ACCOUNT Supplies Expense   ACCOUNT NO. 523

DATE		ITEM	POST. REF.	DEBIT	CREDIT	BALANCE	
						DEBIT	CREDIT

ACCOUNT Insurance Expense   ACCOUNT NO. 535

DATE		ITEM	POST. REF.	DEBIT	CREDIT	BALANCE	
						DEBIT	CREDIT

ACCOUNT Depreciation Expense—Van   ACCOUNT NO. 541

DATE		ITEM	POST. REF.	DEBIT	CREDIT	BALANCE	
						DEBIT	CREDIT

Problem 5-17A: See pages 130 and 131

Exercise 5-1B

(Balance Sheet) Supplies	(Income Statement) Supplies Expense

GENERAL JOURNAL

PAGE

	DATE	DESCRIPTION	POST. REF.	DEBIT	CREDIT	
1						1
2						2
3						3
4						4
5						5
6						6

Exercise 5-2B

(Balance Sheet) Prepaid Insurance	(Income Statement) Insurance Expense

GENERAL JOURNAL

PAGE

	DATE	DESCRIPTION	POST. REF.	DEBIT	CREDIT	
1						1
2						2
3						3
4						4
5						5
6						6

Problem 5-17A

Joyce Lee's

Work

For Month Ended

	ACCOUNT TITLE	TRIAL BALANCE										ADJUSTMENTS							
		DEBIT					CREDIT					DEBIT				CREDIT			
1	Cash	1	7	2	5	00													
2	Accounts Receivable		9	6	0	00													
3	Supplies		5	2	5	00													
4	Prepaid Insurance		9	3	0	00													
5	Office Equipment	5	4	5	0	00													
6	Accum. Depr.—Office Equipment																		
7	Accounts Payable							4	8	0	00								
8	Wages Payable																		
9	Joyce Lee, Capital						7	5	0	0	00								
10	Joyce Lee, Drawing	1	1	2	5	00													
11	Professional Fees						5	7	0	0	00								
12	Wages Expense	1	4	2	0	00													
13	Advertising Expense		3	5	0	00													
14	Rent Expense		7	0	0	00													
15	Supplies Expense																		
16	Phone Expense		1	3	0	00													
17	Utilities Expense		1	9	0	00													
18	Insurance Expense																		
19	Depr. Expense—Office Equipment																		
20	Miscellaneous Expense		1	7	5	00													
21		13	6	8	0	00	13	6	8	0	00								
22																			
23																			
24																			
25																			
26																			
27																			
28																			
29																			
30																			
31																			

Problem 5-17A (Concluded)

Tax Service

Sheet

March 31, 20--

ADJUSTED TRIAL BALANCE		INCOME STATEMENT		BALANCE SHEET		
DEBIT	CREDIT	DEBIT	CREDIT	DEBIT	CREDIT	
						1
						2
						3
						4
						5
						6
						7
						8
						9
						10
						11
						12
						13
						14
						15
						16
						17
						18
						19
						20
						21
						22
						23
						24
						25
						26
						27
						28
						29
						30
						31

Exercise 5-3B

(Income Statement) Wages Expense	(Balance Sheet) Wages Payable

GENERAL JOURNAL

PAGE

	DATE	DESCRIPTION	POST. REF.	DEBIT	CREDIT	
1						1
2						2
3						3
4						4

Exercise 5-4B

_____

_____

_____

(Income Statement) Depr. Expense—Delivery Equipment	(Balance Sheet) Accum. Depr.—Delivery Equipment

GENERAL JOURNAL

PAGE

	DATE	DESCRIPTION	POST. REF.	DEBIT	CREDIT	
1						1
2						2
3						3
4						4

Exercise 5-5B

_____

_____

Exercise 5-6B

1.

(Balance Sheet) Supplies		(Income Statement) Supplies Expense
TB	540	
Bal.	_____	

2.

(Balance Sheet) Supplies		(Income Statement) Supplies Expense
TB	330	
Bal.	_____	

Exercise 5-7B

1.

(Balance Sheet) Prepaid Insurance		(Income Statement) Insurance Expense
TB	960	
Bal.	_____	

2.

(Balance Sheet) Prepaid Insurance		(Income Statement) Insurance Expense
TB	1,135	
Bal.	_____	

Exercise 5-8B

GENERAL JOURNAL

PAGE 7

	DATE		DESCRIPTION	POST. REF.	DEBIT	CREDIT	
1			Adjusting Entries				1
2	20-- July	31	Insurance Expense		3 2 0 00		2
3			Prepaid Insurance			3 2 0 00	3
4							4
5		31	Depreciation Expense—Cleaning Equipment		1 4 5 00		5
6			Accumulated Depreciation—Cleaning Equipment			1 4 5 00	6
7							7
8							8
9							9
10							10
11							11
12							12
13							13
14							14
15							15
16							16

Exercise 5-8B (Concluded)

GENERAL LEDGER

ACCOUNT   Prepaid Insurance   ACCOUNT NO.   145

DATE		ITEM	POST. REF.	DEBIT	CREDIT	BALANCE	
						DEBIT	CREDIT
20-- July	1	Balance	✓			3 2 0 00	
	15		J6	6 4 0 00		9 6 0 00	

ACCOUNT   Accumulated Depreciation—Cleaning Equipment   ACCOUNT NO.   183.1

DATE		ITEM	POST. REF.	DEBIT	CREDIT	BALANCE	
						DEBIT	CREDIT
20-- July	1	Balance	✓				8 7 0 00

ACCOUNT   Insurance Expense   ACCOUNT NO.   535

DATE		ITEM	POST. REF.	DEBIT	CREDIT	BALANCE	
						DEBIT	CREDIT

ACCOUNT   Depreciation Expense—Cleaning Equipment   ACCOUNT NO.   541

DATE		ITEM	POST. REF.	DEBIT	CREDIT	BALANCE	
						DEBIT	CREDIT

Exercise 5-9B

Jasmine Kah's Auto Detailing

Work Sheet (Partial)

For Month Ended June 30, 20--

	ACCOUNT TITLE	TRIAL BALANCE DEBIT	TRIAL BALANCE CREDIT	ADJUSTMENTS DEBIT	ADJUSTMENTS CREDIT	ADJUSTED TRIAL BALANCE DEBIT	ADJUSTED TRIAL BALANCE CREDIT
1	Cash	1 5 0 00				1 5 0 00	
2	Supplies	5 2 0 00				9 0 00	
3	Prepaid Insurance	7 5 0 00				2 0 0 00	
4	Cleaning Equipment	5 4 0 0 00				5 4 0 0 00	
5	Accum. Depr.—Cleaning Equip.		8 5 0 00				1 1 5 0 00
6	Wages Payable						2 5 0 00
7	Jasmine Kah, Capital		4 6 0 0 00				4 6 0 0 00
8	Detailing Fees		2 2 2 0 00				2 2 2 0 00
9	Wages Expense	7 0 0 00				9 5 0 00	
10	Advertising Expense	1 5 0 00				1 5 0 00	
11	Supplies Expense					4 3 0 00	
12	Insurance Expense					5 5 0 00	
13	Depr. Exp.—Cleaning Equip.					3 0 0 00	
14		7 6 7 0 00	7 6 7 0 00			8 2 2 0 00	8 2 2 0 00
15							
16							
17							
18							
19							
20							
21							
22							
23							
24							
25							

Exercise 5-10B

GENERAL JOURNAL   PAGE

	DATE		DESCRIPTION	POST. REF.	DEBIT	CREDIT	
1							1
2							2
3							3
4							4
5							5
6							6
7							7
8							8
9							9
10							10
11							11
12							12
13							13
14							14
15							15

Exercise 5-11B

	Income Statement		Balance Sheet	
	Debit	**Credit**	**Debit**	**Credit**
Cash	_____	_____	_____	_____
Accounts Receivable	_____	_____	_____	_____
Supplies	_____	_____	_____	_____
Prepaid Insurance	_____	_____	_____	_____
Automobile	_____	_____	_____	_____
Accum. Depr.—Automobile	_____	_____	_____	_____
Accounts Payable	_____	_____	_____	_____
Wages Payable	_____	_____	_____	_____
Owner, Capital	_____	_____	_____	_____
Owner, Drawing	_____	_____	_____	_____
Service Fees	_____	_____	_____	_____
Wages Expense	_____	_____	_____	_____
Supplies Expense	_____	_____	_____	_____
Utilities Expense	_____	_____	_____	_____
Insurance Expense	_____	_____	_____	_____
Depr. Exp.—Automobile	_____	_____	_____	_____

Exercise 5-12B

	Income Statement		Balance Sheet	
	Debit	**Credit**	**Debit**	**Credit**
Net Income	_____	_____	_____	_____
Net Loss	_____	_____	_____	_____

Exercise 5-13B

	Cash Basis	Modified Cash Basis	Accrual Basis

1. Office Equipment
    Cash
        Purchased equipment for cash			

2. Office Equipment
    Accounts Payable
        Purchased equipment on account			

3. Cash
    Revenue
        Cash receipts for week			

4. Accounts Receivable
    Revenue
        Services performed on account			

5. Prepaid Insurance
    Cash
        Purchased prepaid asset			

6. Supplies
    Accounts Payable
        Purchased prepaid asset			

7. Phone Expense
    Cash
        Paid phone bill			

8. Wages Expense
    Cash
        Paid wages for month			

9. Accounts Payable
    Cash
        Made payment on account			

10. Supplies Expense Supplies			

Exercise 5-13B (Concluded)

	Cash Basis	Modified Cash Basis	Accrual Basis
11. Wages Expense Wages Payable			
12. Depreciation Expense—Office Equipment Accum. Depr.—Office Equipment			

This page intentionally left blank.

Problem 5-14B

Louie's Lawn

Work

For Month Ended

	ACCOUNT TITLE	TRIAL BALANCE										ADJUSTMENTS								
		DEBIT					CREDIT					DEBIT					CREDIT			
1	Cash	1	3	7	5	00														
2	Accounts Receivable		8	8	0	00														
3	Supplies		4	9	0	00														
4	Prepaid Insurance		8	0	0	00														
5	Lawn Equipment	5	7	0	0	00														
6	Accum. Depr.—Lawn Equipment																			
7	Accounts Payable							7	8	0	00									
8	Wages Payable																			
9	Louie Long, Capital						6	5	0	0	00									
10	Louie Long, Drawing	1	2	5	0	00														
11	Lawn Service Fees						6	1	0	0	00									
12	Wages Expense	1	1	4	5	00														
13	Advertising Expense		5	4	0	00														
14	Rent Expense		7	2	5	00														
15	Supplies Expense																			
16	Phone Expense		1	6	0	00														
17	Insurance Expense																			
18	Repair Expense		2	5	0	00														
19	Depr. Expense—Lawn Equipment																			
20	Miscellaneous Expense			6	5	00														
21		13	3	8	0	00	13	3	8	0	00									
22																				
23																				
24																				
25																				
26																				
27																				
28																				
29																				
30																				
31																				
32																				
33																				

Problem 5-14B (Concluded)

Service

Sheet

March 31, 20--

ADJUSTED TRIAL BALANCE		INCOME STATEMENT		BALANCE SHEET		
DEBIT	CREDIT	DEBIT	CREDIT	DEBIT	CREDIT	
						1
						2
						3
						4
						5
						6
						7
						8
						9
						10
						11
						12
						13
						14
						15
						16
						17
						18
						19
						20
						21
						22
						23
						24
						25
						26
						27
						28
						29
						30
						31
						32
						33

Problem 5-15B

Nolan's Home

Work

For Month Ended

	ACCOUNT TITLE	TRIAL BALANCE											ADJUSTMENTS											
		DEBIT						CREDIT						DEBIT						CREDIT					
1	Cash		8	3	0	00																			
2	Accounts Receivable		7	6	0	00																			
3	Supplies		6	2	5	00																			
4	Prepaid Insurance		9	5	0	00																			
5	Automobile	6	5	0	0	00																			
6	Accum. Depr.—Automobile																								
7	Accounts Payable							1	5	0	0	00													
8	Wages Payable																								
9	Val Nolan, Capital							9	9	0	0	00													
10	Val Nolan, Drawing	1	1	0	0	00																			
11	Appraisal Fees							3	0	0	0	00													
12	Wages Expense	1	5	6	0	00																			
13	Advertising Expense		4	2	0	00																			
14	Rent Expense	1	0	5	0	00																			
15	Supplies Expense																								
16	Phone Expense		2	5	5	00																			
17	Insurance Expense																								
18	Repair Expense		2	7	0	00																			
19	Oil and Gas Expense			8	0	00																			
20	Depr. Expense—Automobile																								
21		14	4	0	0	00		14	4	0	0	00													
22																									
23																									
24																									
25																									
26																									
27																									
28																									
29																									
30																									
31																									
32																									
33																									

Problem 5-15B (Concluded)

Appraisals _____

Sheet _____

October 31, 20-- _____

	ADJUSTED TRIAL BALANCE		INCOME STATEMENT		BALANCE SHEET		
	DEBIT	CREDIT	DEBIT	CREDIT	DEBIT	CREDIT	
1							1
2							2
3							3
4							4
5							5
6							6
7							7
8							8
9							9
10							10
11							11
12							12
13							13
14							14
15							15
16							16
17							17
18							18
19							19
20							20
21							21
22							22
23							23
24							24
25							25
26							26
27							27
28							28
29							29
30							30
31							31
32							32
33							33

Problem 5-16B

1.

GENERAL JOURNAL

	DATE		DESCRIPTION	POST. REF.	DEBIT	CREDIT	
1							1
2							2
3							3
4							4
5							5
6							6
7							7
8							8
9							9
10							10
11							11
12							12
13							13
14							14
15							15
16							16
17							17
18							18
19							19
20							20
21							21
22							22
23							23
24							24
25							25
26							26
27							27
28							28
29							29
30							30
31							31
32							32
33							33
34							34
35							35
36							36

Problem 5-16B (Continued)

2.   **GENERAL LEDGER**

ACCOUNT   Supplies   ACCOUNT NO.   141

DATE		ITEM	POST. REF.	DEBIT	CREDIT	BALANCE DEBIT	BALANCE CREDIT
20-- Oct.	2		J1	6 2 5 00		6 2 5 00	

ACCOUNT   Prepaid Insurance   ACCOUNT NO.   145

DATE		ITEM	POST. REF.	DEBIT	CREDIT	BALANCE DEBIT	BALANCE CREDIT
20-- Oct.	3		J1	9 5 0 00		9 5 0 00	

ACCOUNT   Accumulated Depreciation—Automobile   ACCOUNT NO.   185.1

DATE	ITEM	POST. REF.	DEBIT	CREDIT	BALANCE DEBIT	BALANCE CREDIT

Problem 5-16B (Continued)

ACCOUNT   Wages Payable   ACCOUNT NO.   219

DATE		ITEM	POST. REF.	DEBIT	CREDIT	BALANCE	
						DEBIT	CREDIT

ACCOUNT   Wages Expense   ACCOUNT NO.   511

DATE		ITEM	POST. REF.	DEBIT	CREDIT	BALANCE	
						DEBIT	CREDIT
20-- Oct.	15		J2	7 0 0 00		7 0 0 00	
	26		J2	8 6 0 00		1 5 6 0 00	

ACCOUNT   Supplies Expense   ACCOUNT NO.   523

DATE		ITEM	POST. REF.	DEBIT	CREDIT	BALANCE	
						DEBIT	CREDIT

Problem 5-16B (Concluded)

ACCOUNT Insurance Expense   ACCOUNT NO. 535

DATE	ITEM	POST. REF.	DEBIT	CREDIT	BALANCE	
					DEBIT	CREDIT

ACCOUNT Depreciation Expense—Automobile   ACCOUNT NO. 541

DATE	ITEM	POST. REF.	DEBIT	CREDIT	BALANCE	
					DEBIT	CREDIT

Problem 5-17B

Dick Ady's

Work

For Month Ended

	ACCOUNT TITLE	TRIAL BALANCE								ADJUSTMENTS							
		DEBIT					CREDIT				DEBIT				CREDIT			
1	Cash	1	3	6	5	00												
2	Accounts Receivable		8	4	5	00												
3	Supplies		6	2	0	00												
4	Prepaid Insurance	1	1	5	0	00												
5	Office Equipment	6	4	0	0	00												
6	Accum. Depr.—Office Equipment																	
7	Accounts Payable							7	3	5	00							
8	Wages Payable																	
9	Dick Ady, Capital						7	8	0	0	00							
10	Dick Ady, Drawing	1	2	0	0	00												
11	Professional Fees						6	3	5	0	00							
12	Wages Expense	1	4	9	5	00												
13	Advertising Expense		3	8	0	00												
14	Rent Expense		8	5	0	00												
15	Supplies Expense																	
16	Phone Expense		2	0	5	00												
17	Utilities Expense		2	8	5	00												
18	Insurance Expense																	
19	Depr. Expense—Office Equipment																	
20	Miscellaneous Expense			9	0	00												
21		14	8	8	5	00	14	8	8	5	00							
22																		
23																		
24																		
25																		
26																		
27																		
28																		
29																		
30																		
31																		
32																		

Problem 5-17B (Concluded)

Bookkeeping Service

Sheet

July 31, 20--

ADJUSTED TRIAL BALANCE		INCOME STATEMENT		BALANCE SHEET		
DEBIT	CREDIT	DEBIT	CREDIT	DEBIT	CREDIT	
						1
						2
						3
						4
						5
						6
						7
						8
						9
						10
						11
						12
						13
						14
						15
						16
						17
						18
						19
						20
						21
						22
						23
						24
						25
						26
						27
						28
						29
						30
						31
						32

Mastery Problem

1.

Kristi Williams Family

Work

For Year Ended

	ACCOUNT TITLE	TRIAL BALANCE										ADJUSTMENTS									
		DEBIT					CREDIT					DEBIT					CREDIT				
1	Cash	8	7	3	0	00															
2	Office Supplies		7	0	0	00															
3	Prepaid Insurance		6	0	0	00															
4	Office Equipment	18	0	0	0	00															
5																					
6	Computer Equipment	6	0	0	0	00															
7																					
8	Notes Payable						8	0	0	0	00										
9	Accounts Payable							5	0	0	00										
10	Kristi Williams, Capital						11	4	0	0	00										
11	Kristi Williams, Drawing	3	0	0	0	00															
12	Client Fees						35	8	0	0	00										
13	Wages Expense	9	5	0	0	00															
14	Rent Expense	6	0	0	0	00															
15																					
16	Utilities Expense	2	1	7	0	00															
17																					
18																					
19																					
20	Miscellaneous Expense	1	0	0	0	00															
21		55	7	0	0	00	55	7	0	0	00										
22																					
23																					
24																					
25																					
26																					
27																					
28																					
29																					
30																					
31																					
32																					

Mastery Problem (Continued)

Counseling Services

Sheet

December 31, 20--

ADJUSTED TRIAL BALANCE		INCOME STATEMENT		BALANCE SHEET		
DEBIT	CREDIT	DEBIT	CREDIT	DEBIT	CREDIT	
						1
						2
						3
						4
						5
						6
						7
						8
						9
						10
						11
						12
						13
						14
						15
						16
						17
						18
						19
						20
						21
						22
						23
						24
						25
						26
						27
						28
						29
						30
						31
						32

Mastery Problem (Concluded)

2.

GENERAL JOURNAL

	DATE	DESCRIPTION	POST. REF.	DEBIT	CREDIT	
1						1
2						2
3						3
4						4
5						5
6						6
7						7
8						8
9						9
10						10
11						11
12						12
13						13
14						14
15						15
16						16
17						17
18						18
19						19
20						20
21						21
22						22
23						23
24						24
25						25
26						26
27						27
28						28
29						29
30						30
31						31
32						32
33						33
34						34
35						35

Challenge Problem

See pages 156–157 for work sheet for Challenge Problem.

Challenge Problem

1.

Diane Kiefner's Wilderness

Work

For Summer

	ACCOUNT TITLE	TRIAL BALANCE											ADJUSTMENTS										
		DEBIT					CREDIT						DEBIT					CREDIT					
1	Cash	11	5	0	0	00																	
2																							
3																							
4																							
5	Diane Kiefner, Capital						15	0	0	0	00												
6	Tour Revenue						10	0	0	0	00												
7	Advertising Supplies Expense	1	0	0	0	00																	
8	Food Expense	2	0	0	0	00																	
9	Equipment Rental Expense	3	0	0	0	00																	
10	Travel Expense	4	0	0	0	00																	
11	Kayak Expense	3	5	0	0	00																	
12																							
13		25	0	0	0	00	25	0	0	0	00												
14																							
15																							
16																							
17																							
18																							
19																							

Challenge Problem (Concluded)

Kayaking Tours _____

Sheet _____

Ended 20-- _____

ADJUSTED TRIAL BALANCE		INCOME STATEMENT		BALANCE SHEET		
DEBIT	CREDIT	DEBIT	CREDIT	DEBIT	CREDIT	
						1
						2
						3
						4
						5
						6
						7
						8
						9
						10
						11
						12
						13
						14
						15
						16
						17
						18
						19

2. _____

APPENDIX: DEPRECIATION METHODS

Exercise 5Apx-1A

Straight-Line Depreciation

Year	Depreciable Cost	×	Rate	=	Depreciation Expense	Accumulated Depreciation End of Year	Book Value End of Year
—	—		—		—	—	—
—	—		—		—	—	—
—	—		—		—	—	—
—	—		—		—	—	—

Exercise 5Apx-2A

Sum-of-the-Years'-Digits

Year	Depreciable Cost	×	Rate	=	Depreciation Expense	Accumulated Depreciation End of Year	Book Value End of Year
—	—		—		—	—	—
—	—		—		—	—	—
—	—		—		—	—	—
—	—		—		—	—	—

Exercise 5Apx-3A

Double-Declining-Balance Method

Year	Book Value Beginning of Year	×	Rate	=	Depreciation Expense	Accumulated Depreciation End of Year	Book Value End of Year
—	—		—		—	—	—
—	—		—		—	—	—
—	—		—		—	—	—
—	—		—		—	—	—

Exercise 5Apx-4A

Modified Accelerated Cost Recovery System

Year	Cost	×	Rate	=	Depreciation Expense	Accumulated Depreciation End of Year	Book Value End of Year

Exercise 5Apx-1B

Straight-Line Depreciation

Year	Depreciable Cost	×	Rate	=	Depreciation Expense	Accumulated Depreciation End of Year	Book Value End of Year

Exercise 5Apx-2B

Sum-of-the-Years'-Digits

Year	Depreciable Cost	×	Rate	=	Depreciation Expense	Accumulated Depreciation End of Year	Book Value End of Year

Exercise 5Apx-3B

Double-Declining-Balance Method

Year	Book Value Beginning of Year	×	Rate	=	Depreciation Expense	Accumulated Depreciation End of Year	Book Value End of Year

Exercise 5Apx-4B

Modified Accelerated Cost Recovery System

Year	Cost	×	Rate	=	Depreciation Expense	Accumulated Depreciation End of Year	Book Value End of Year

Exercise 6-1A

Exercise 6-2A

Exercise 6-3A

Exercise 6-4A

GENERAL JOURNAL   PAGE 1

	DATE		DESCRIPTION	POST. REF.	DEBIT	CREDIT	
1							1
2							2
3							3
4							4
5							5
6							6
7							7
8							8
9							9
10							10
11							11
12							12
13							13
14							14
15							15
16							16
17							17
18							18
19							19
20							20
21							21
22							22
23							23

Exercise 6-4A (Concluded)

Exercise 6-5A

GENERAL JOURNAL

	DATE	DESCRIPTION	POST. REF.	DEBIT	CREDIT	
1						1
2						2
3						3
4						4
5						5
6						6
7						7
8						8
9						9
10						10
11						11
12						12
13						13
14						14
15						15
16						16
17						17
18						18
19						19
20						20
21						21
22						22
23						23
24						24
25						25
26						26
27						27
28						28
29						29
30						30
31						31
32						32
33						33
34						34
35						35
36						36

Exercise 6-5A (Concluded)

Cash		101
Bal.	500	

Advertising Expense		512
Bal.	200	

Accounts Receivable		122
Bal.	1,500	

Travel Expense		515
Bal.	600	

Wages Payable		219
	Bal.	400

Supplies Expense		524
Bal.	500	

Chris Williams, Capital		311
	Bal.	9,000

Insurance Expense		535
Bal.	100	

Chris Williams, Drawing		312
Bal.	1,000	

Postage Expense		536
Bal.	50	

Income Summary		313

Gas and Oil Expense		538
Bal.	150	

Golf Instruction Fees		401
	Bal.	4,000

Miscellaneous Expense		549
Bal.	80	

Wages Expense		511
Bal.	800	

Exercise 6-6A

GENERAL JOURNAL

PAGE _____

	DATE		DESCRIPTION	POST. REF.	DEBIT	CREDIT	
1							1
2							2
3							3
4							4
5							5
6							6
7							7
8							8
9							9
10							10
11							11
12							12
13							13
14							14
15							15
16							16
17							17
18							18
19							19
20							20
21							21
22							22
23							23
24							24
25							25
26							26
27							27
28							28
29							29
30							30
31							31
32							32
33							33
34							34
35							35
36							36

Exercise 6-6A (Concluded)

Accum. Depr.—Delivery Equip.	185.1		Wages Payable	219
	Bal.	100		Bal.	200

Saburo Goto, Capital	311		Saburo Goto, Drawing	312
	Bal.	4,000	Bal.	800	

Income Summary	313		Delivery Fees	401
				Bal.	2,200

Wages Expense	511		Advertising Expense	512
Bal.	1,800		Bal.	80	

Rent Expense	521		Supplies Expense	523
Bal.	500		Bal.	120	

Phone Expense	525		Electricity Expense	533
Bal.	58		Bal.	44	

Insurance Expense	535		Gas and Oil Expense	538
Bal.	30		Bal.	38	

Depr. Exp.—Delivery Equip.	541		Miscellaneous Expense	549
Bal.	100		Bal.	33	

Problem 6-7A

1.

_____

2.

_____

Problem 6-7A (Concluded)

3.

Problem 6-8A

1.

GENERAL JOURNAL

PAGE 10

	DATE		DESCRIPTION	POST. REF.	DEBIT	CREDIT	
1							1
2							2
3							3
4							4
5							5
6							6
7							7
8							8
9							9
10							10
11							11
12							12
13							13
14							14
15							15
16							16
17							17
18							18

Problem 6-8A (Continued)

2.

GENERAL JOURNAL

PAGE 11

	DATE	DESCRIPTION	POST. REF.	DEBIT	CREDIT	
1						1
2						2
3						3
4						4
5						5
6						6
7						7
8						8
9						9
10						10
11						11
12						12
13						13
14						14
15						15
16						16
17						17
18						18
19						19
20						20
21						21
22						22
23						23

1. and 2.

GENERAL LEDGER

ACCOUNT Cash

ACCOUNT NO. 101

DATE		ITEM	POST. REF.	DEBIT	CREDIT	BALANCE DEBIT	BALANCE CREDIT
20-- Jan.	31	Balance	✓			3 6 7 3 00	

Problem 6-8A (Continued)

ACCOUNT Accounts Receivable   ACCOUNT NO. 122

DATE	ITEM	POST. REF.	DEBIT	CREDIT	BALANCE DEBIT	BALANCE CREDIT
20-- Jan. 31	Balance	✓			1 4 5 0 00	

ACCOUNT Supplies   ACCOUNT NO. 141

DATE	ITEM	POST. REF.	DEBIT	CREDIT	BALANCE DEBIT	BALANCE CREDIT
20-- Jan. 31	Balance	✓			7 0 0 00	

ACCOUNT Prepaid Insurance   ACCOUNT NO. 145

DATE	ITEM	POST. REF.	DEBIT	CREDIT	BALANCE DEBIT	BALANCE CREDIT
20-- Jan. 31	Balance	✓			9 0 0 00	

ACCOUNT Delivery Equipment   ACCOUNT NO. 185

DATE	ITEM	POST. REF.	DEBIT	CREDIT	BALANCE DEBIT	BALANCE CREDIT
20-- Jan. 31	Balance	✓			3 2 0 0 00	

ACCOUNT Accumulated Depreciation—Delivery Equipment   ACCOUNT NO. 185.1

DATE	ITEM	POST. REF.	DEBIT	CREDIT	BALANCE DEBIT	BALANCE CREDIT

Problem 6-8A (Continued)

ACCOUNT Accounts Payable   ACCOUNT NO. 202

DATE		ITEM	POST. REF.	DEBIT	CREDIT	BALANCE	
						DEBIT	CREDIT
20-- Jan.	31	Balance	✓				1 2 0 0 00

ACCOUNT Wages Payable   ACCOUNT NO. 219

DATE		ITEM	POST. REF.	DEBIT	CREDIT	BALANCE	
						DEBIT	CREDIT

ACCOUNT Don Megaffin, Capital   ACCOUNT NO. 311

DATE		ITEM	POST. REF.	DEBIT	CREDIT	BALANCE	
						DEBIT	CREDIT
20-- Jan.	31	Balance	✓				8 0 0 0 00

ACCOUNT Don Megaffin, Drawing   ACCOUNT NO. 312

DATE		ITEM	POST. REF.	DEBIT	CREDIT	BALANCE	
						DEBIT	CREDIT
20-- Jan.	31	Balance	✓			1 1 0 0 00	

ACCOUNT Income Summary   ACCOUNT NO. 313

DATE	ITEM	POST. REF.	DEBIT	CREDIT	BALANCE	
					DEBIT	CREDIT

Name _____

Problem 6-8A (Continued)

ACCOUNT Repair Fees   ACCOUNT NO. 401

DATE		ITEM	POST. REF.	DEBIT	CREDIT	BALANCE	
						DEBIT	CREDIT
20-- Jan.	31	Balance	✓				4 7 0 0 00

ACCOUNT Wages Expense   ACCOUNT NO. 511

DATE		ITEM	POST. REF.	DEBIT	CREDIT	BALANCE	
						DEBIT	CREDIT
20-- Jan.	31	Balance	✓			1 7 5 0 00	

ACCOUNT Advertising Expense   ACCOUNT NO. 512

DATE		ITEM	POST. REF.	DEBIT	CREDIT	BALANCE	
						DEBIT	CREDIT
20-- Jan.	31	Balance	✓			2 0 0 00	

ACCOUNT Rent Expense   ACCOUNT NO. 521

DATE		ITEM	POST. REF.	DEBIT	CREDIT	BALANCE	
						DEBIT	CREDIT
20-- Jan.	31	Balance	✓			6 4 0 00	

ACCOUNT Supplies Expense   ACCOUNT NO. 523

DATE		ITEM	POST. REF.	DEBIT	CREDIT	BALANCE	
						DEBIT	CREDIT

Problem 6-8A (Continued)

ACCOUNT Phone Expense   ACCOUNT NO. 525

DATE		ITEM	POST. REF.	DEBIT	CREDIT	BALANCE	
						DEBIT	CREDIT
20-- Jan.	31	Balance	✓			5 0 00	

ACCOUNT Insurance Expense   ACCOUNT NO. 535

DATE		ITEM	POST. REF.	DEBIT	CREDIT	BALANCE	
						DEBIT	CREDIT

ACCOUNT Gas and Oil Expense   ACCOUNT NO. 538

DATE		ITEM	POST. REF.	DEBIT	CREDIT	BALANCE	
						DEBIT	CREDIT
20-- Jan.	31	Balance	✓			2 0 0 00	

ACCOUNT Depreciation Expense—Delivery Equipment   ACCOUNT NO. 541

DATE		ITEM	POST. REF.	DEBIT	CREDIT	BALANCE	
						DEBIT	CREDIT

ACCOUNT Miscellaneous Expense   ACCOUNT NO. 549

DATE		ITEM	POST. REF.	DEBIT	CREDIT	BALANCE	
						DEBIT	CREDIT
20-- Jan.	31	Balance	✓			3 7 00	

Problem 6-8A (Concluded)

3.

ACCOUNT TITLE	ACCT. NO.	DEBIT BALANCE	CREDIT BALANCE

Problem 6-9A

Exercise 6-1B

Exercise 6-2B

Exercise 6-3B

Exercise 6-4B

GENERAL JOURNAL

	DATE	DESCRIPTION	POST. REF.	DEBIT	CREDIT	
1						1
2						2
3						3
4						4
5						5
6						6
7						7
8						8
9						9
10						10
11						11
12						12
13						13
14						14
15						15
16						16
17						17
18						18
19						19
20						20
21						21
22						22
23						23

Exercise 6-4B (Concluded)

Exercise 6-5B

GENERAL JOURNAL

	DATE		DESCRIPTION	POST. REF.	DEBIT	CREDIT	
1							1
2							2
3							3
4							4
5							5
6							6
7							7
8							8
9							9
10							10
11							11
12							12
13							13
14							14
15							15
16							16
17							17
18							18
19							19
20							20
21							21
22							22
23							23
24							24
25							25
26							26
27							27
28							28
29							29
30							30
31							31
32							32
33							33
34							34
35							35
36							36

Exercise 6-5B (Concluded)

Cash	101		Advertising Expense	512
Bal. 600			Bal. 600	

Accounts Receivable	122		Travel Expense	515
Bal. 1,800			Bal. 100	

Wages Payable	219		Supplies Expense	524
	Bal. 500		Bal. 900	

Mark Thrasher, Capital	311		Insurance Expense	535
	Bal. 8,000		Bal. 300	

Mark Thrasher, Drawing	312		Postage Expense	536
Bal. 800			Bal. 40	

Income Summary	313		Gas and Oil Expense	538
			Bal. 700	

Lawn Service Fees	401		Miscellaneous Expense	549
	Bal. 5,000		Bal. 200	

Wages Expense	511
Bal. 400	

Exercise 6-6B

	GENERAL JOURNAL			PAGE	

	DATE		DESCRIPTION	POST. REF.	DEBIT	CREDIT	
1							1
2							2
3							3
4							4
5							5
6							6
7							7
8							8
9							9
10							10
11							11
12							12
13							13
14							14
15							15
16							16
17							17
18							18
19							19
20							20
21							21
22							22
23							23
24							24
25							25
26							26
27							27
28							28
29							29
30							30
31							31
32							32
33							33
34							34
35							35
36							36

Exercise 6-6B (Concluded)

Accum. Depr.—Office Equip.	181.1		Wages Payable	219
	Bal.	110		Bal.	260

Raquel Zapata, Capital	311		Raquel Zapata, Drawing	312
	Bal.	6,000	Bal.	2,000	

Income Summary	313		Referral Fees	401
				Bal.	2,813

Wages Expense	511		Advertising Expense	512
Bal.	1,080		Bal.	34	

Rent Expense	521		Supplies Expense	523
Bal.	900		Bal.	322	

Phone Expense	525		Utilities Expense	533
Bal.	133		Bal.	102	

Insurance Expense	535		Gas and Oil Expense	538
Bal.	120		Bal.	88	

Depr. Exp.—Office Equip.	541		Miscellaneous Expense	549
Bal.	110		Bal.	98	

Problem 6-7B

1.

2.

Problem 6-7B (Concluded)

3.

Problem 6-8B

1.

GENERAL JOURNAL

	DATE		DESCRIPTION	POST. REF.	DEBIT	CREDIT	
1							1
2							2
3							3
4							4
5							5
6							6
7							7
8							8
9							9
10							10
11							11
12							12
13							13
14							14
15							15
16							16
17							17
18							18

Problem 6-8B (Continued)

2.

GENERAL JOURNAL

PAGE 11

	DATE	DESCRIPTION	POST. REF.	DEBIT	CREDIT	
1						1
2						2
3						3
4						4
5						5
6						6
7						7
8						8
9						9
10						10
11						11
12						12
13						13
14						14
15						15
16						16
17						17
18						18
19						19
20						20
21						21
22						22
23						23

1. and 2.

GENERAL LEDGER

ACCOUNT   Cash   ACCOUNT NO.   101

DATE	ITEM	POST. REF.	DEBIT	CREDIT	BALANCE DEBIT	BALANCE CREDIT
20-- June 30	Balance	✓			5 2 8 5 00	

Problem 6-8B (Continued)

ACCOUNT   Accounts Receivable   ACCOUNT NO.   122

DATE		ITEM	POST. REF.	DEBIT	CREDIT	BALANCE	
						DEBIT	CREDIT
20-- June	30	Balance	✓			1 0 7 5 00	

ACCOUNT   Supplies   ACCOUNT NO.   141

DATE		ITEM	POST. REF.	DEBIT	CREDIT	BALANCE	
						DEBIT	CREDIT
20-- June	30	Balance	✓			7 5 0 00	

ACCOUNT   Prepaid Insurance   ACCOUNT NO.   145

DATE		ITEM	POST. REF.	DEBIT	CREDIT	BALANCE	
						DEBIT	CREDIT
20-- June	30	Balance	✓			5 0 0 00	

ACCOUNT   Office Equipment   ACCOUNT NO.   181

DATE		ITEM	POST. REF.	DEBIT	CREDIT	BALANCE	
						DEBIT	CREDIT
20-- June	30	Balance	✓			2 2 0 0 00	

ACCOUNT   Accumulated Depreciation—Office Equipment   ACCOUNT NO.   181.1

DATE		ITEM	POST. REF.	DEBIT	CREDIT	BALANCE	
						DEBIT	CREDIT

Problem 6-8B (Continued)

ACCOUNT Accounts Payable   ACCOUNT NO. 202

DATE		ITEM	POST. REF.	DEBIT	CREDIT	BALANCE	
						DEBIT	CREDIT
20-- June	30	Balance	✓				1 5 0 0 00

ACCOUNT Wages Payable   ACCOUNT NO. 219

DATE		ITEM	POST. REF.	DEBIT	CREDIT	BALANCE	
						DEBIT	CREDIT

ACCOUNT Juanita Alvarez, Capital   ACCOUNT NO. 311

DATE		ITEM	POST. REF.	DEBIT	CREDIT	BALANCE	
						DEBIT	CREDIT
20-- June	30	Balance	✓				7 0 0 0 00

ACCOUNT Juanita Alvarez, Drawing   ACCOUNT NO. 312

DATE		ITEM	POST. REF.	DEBIT	CREDIT	BALANCE	
						DEBIT	CREDIT
20-- June	30	Balance	✓			8 0 0 00	

ACCOUNT Income Summary   ACCOUNT NO. 313

DATE		ITEM	POST. REF.	DEBIT	CREDIT	BALANCE	
						DEBIT	CREDIT

Problem 6-8B (Continued)

ACCOUNT Consulting Fees   ACCOUNT NO. 401

DATE		ITEM	POST. REF.	DEBIT	CREDIT	BALANCE	
						DEBIT	CREDIT
20-- June	30	Balance	✓				4 2 0 4 00

ACCOUNT Wages Expense   ACCOUNT NO. 511

DATE		ITEM	POST. REF.	DEBIT	CREDIT	BALANCE	
						DEBIT	CREDIT
20-- June	30	Balance	✓			1 4 0 0 00	

ACCOUNT Advertising Expense   ACCOUNT NO. 512

DATE		ITEM	POST. REF.	DEBIT	CREDIT	BALANCE	
						DEBIT	CREDIT
20-- June	30	Balance	✓			6 0 00	

ACCOUNT Rent Expense   ACCOUNT NO. 521

DATE		ITEM	POST. REF.	DEBIT	CREDIT	BALANCE	
						DEBIT	CREDIT
20-- June	30	Balance	✓			5 0 0 00	

ACCOUNT Supplies Expense   ACCOUNT NO. 523

DATE		ITEM	POST. REF.	DEBIT	CREDIT	BALANCE	
						DEBIT	CREDIT

Problem 6-8B (Continued)

ACCOUNT Phone Expense   ACCOUNT NO. 525

DATE	ITEM	POST. REF.	DEBIT	CREDIT	BALANCE DEBIT	BALANCE CREDIT
20-- June 30	Balance	✓			4 6 00	

ACCOUNT Electricity Expense   ACCOUNT NO. 533

DATE	ITEM	POST. REF.	DEBIT	CREDIT	BALANCE DEBIT	BALANCE CREDIT
20-- June 30	Balance	✓			3 9 00	

ACCOUNT Insurance Expense   ACCOUNT NO. 535

DATE	ITEM	POST. REF.	DEBIT	CREDIT	BALANCE DEBIT	BALANCE CREDIT

ACCOUNT Gas and Oil Expense   ACCOUNT NO. 538

DATE	ITEM	POST. REF.	DEBIT	CREDIT	BALANCE DEBIT	BALANCE CREDIT
20-- June 30	Balance	✓			2 8 00	

ACCOUNT Depreciation Expense—Office Equipment   ACCOUNT NO. 541

DATE	ITEM	POST. REF.	DEBIT	CREDIT	BALANCE DEBIT	BALANCE CREDIT

Problem 6-8B (Concluded)

ACCOUNT Miscellaneous Expense   ACCOUNT NO. 549

DATE		ITEM	POST. REF.	DEBIT	CREDIT	BALANCE	
						DEBIT	CREDIT
20-- June	30	Balance	✓			2 1 00	

3.

ACCOUNT TITLE	ACCT. NO.	DEBIT BALANCE	CREDIT BALANCE

Problem 6-9B

Mastery Problem

GENERAL JOURNAL

	DATE	DESCRIPTION	POST. REF.	DEBIT	CREDIT	
1						1
2						2
3						3
4						4
5						5
6						6
7						7
8						8
9						9
10						10
11						11
12						12
13						13
14						14
15						15
16						16
17						17
18						18
19						19
20						20
21						21
22						22
23						23
24						24
25						25
26						26
27						27
28						28
29						29
30						30
31						31
32						32
33						33
34						34
35						35
36						36

Mastery Problem (Continued)

Mastery Problem (Concluded)

Challenge Problem

Challenge Problem (Concluded)

Exercise 6Apx-1A

a. _____   g. _____

b. _____   h. _____

c. _____   i. _____

d. _____   j. _____

e. _____   k. _____

f. _____

Problem 6Apx-2A

_____

_____

_____

Exercise 6Apx-1B

a. _____   g. _____

b. _____   h. _____

c. _____   i. _____

d. _____   j. _____

e. _____   k. _____

f. _____

Problem 6Apx-2B

Comprehensive Problem 1: The Accounting Cycle

1.

GENERAL JOURNAL

PAGE 1

	DATE	DESCRIPTION	POST. REF.	DEBIT	CREDIT	
1						1
2						2
3						3
4						4
5						5
6						6
7						7
8						8
9						9
10						10
11						11
12						12
13						13
14						14
15						15
16						16
17						17
18						18
19						19
20						20
21						21
22						22
23						23
24						24
25						25
26						26
27						27
28						28
29						29
30						30
31						31
32						32
33						33
34						34

Comprehensive Problem 1 (Continued)

GENERAL JOURNAL

	DATE	DESCRIPTION	POST. REF.	DEBIT	CREDIT	
1						1
2						2
3						3
4						4
5						5
6						6
7						7
8						8
9						9
10						10
11						11
12						12
13						13
14						14
15						15
16						16
17						17
18						18
19						19
20						20
21						21
22						22
23						23
24						24
25						25
26						26
27						27
28						28
29						29
30						30
31						31
32						32
33						33
34						34
35						35

Comprehensive Problem 1 (Continued)

GENERAL JOURNAL

	DATE		DESCRIPTION	POST. REF.	DEBIT	CREDIT	
1							1
2							2
3							3
4							4
5							5
6							6
7							7
8							8
9							9
10							10
11							11
12							12
13							13
14							14
15							15
16							16
17							17
18							18
19							19
20							20
21							21
22							22
23							23
24							24
25							25
26							26
27							27
28							28
29							29
30							30
31							31
32							32
33							33
34							34
35							35

Comprehensive Problem 1 (Continued)

GENERAL JOURNAL

PAGE 4

	DATE		DESCRIPTION	POST. REF.	DEBIT	CREDIT	
1							1
2							2
3							3
4							4
5							5
6							6
7							7
8							8
9							9
10							10
11							11

2., 6., and 11.

GENERAL LEDGER

ACCOUNT Cash

ACCOUNT NO. 101

DATE	ITEM	POST. REF.	DEBIT	CREDIT	BALANCE	
					DEBIT	CREDIT

Comprehensive Problem 1 (Continued)

ACCOUNT Office Supplies   ACCOUNT NO. 142

DATE	ITEM	POST. REF.	DEBIT	CREDIT	BALANCE	
					DEBIT	CREDIT

ACCOUNT Food Supplies   ACCOUNT NO. 144

DATE	ITEM	POST. REF.	DEBIT	CREDIT	BALANCE	
					DEBIT	CREDIT

ACCOUNT Prepaid Insurance   ACCOUNT NO. 145

DATE	ITEM	POST. REF.	DEBIT	CREDIT	BALANCE	
					DEBIT	CREDIT

ACCOUNT Fishing Boats   ACCOUNT NO. 181

DATE	ITEM	POST. REF.	DEBIT	CREDIT	BALANCE	
					DEBIT	CREDIT

Comprehensive Problem 1 (Continued)

ACCOUNT Accumulated Depreciation—Fishing Boats   ACCOUNT NO. 181.1

DATE	ITEM	POST. REF.	DEBIT	CREDIT	BALANCE	
					DEBIT	CREDIT

ACCOUNT Accounts Payable   ACCOUNT NO. 202

DATE	ITEM	POST. REF.	DEBIT	CREDIT	BALANCE	
					DEBIT	CREDIT

ACCOUNT Wages Payable   ACCOUNT NO. 219

DATE	ITEM	POST. REF.	DEBIT	CREDIT	BALANCE	
					DEBIT	CREDIT

ACCOUNT Bob Night, Capital   ACCOUNT NO. 311

DATE	ITEM	POST. REF.	DEBIT	CREDIT	BALANCE	
					DEBIT	CREDIT

Comprehensive Problem 1 (Continued)

ACCOUNT Bob Night, Drawing   ACCOUNT NO. 312

DATE	ITEM	POST. REF.	DEBIT	CREDIT	BALANCE DEBIT	BALANCE CREDIT

ACCOUNT Income Summary   ACCOUNT NO. 313

DATE	ITEM	POST. REF.	DEBIT	CREDIT	BALANCE DEBIT	BALANCE CREDIT

ACCOUNT Registration Fees   ACCOUNT NO. 401

DATE	ITEM	POST. REF.	DEBIT	CREDIT	BALANCE DEBIT	BALANCE CREDIT

Comprehensive Problem 1 (Continued)

ACCOUNT   Wages Expense   ACCOUNT NO. 511

DATE	ITEM	POST. REF.	DEBIT	CREDIT	BALANCE	
					DEBIT	CREDIT

ACCOUNT   Rent Expense   ACCOUNT NO. 521

DATE	ITEM	POST. REF.	DEBIT	CREDIT	BALANCE	
					DEBIT	CREDIT

ACCOUNT   Office Supplies Expense   ACCOUNT NO. 523

DATE	ITEM	POST. REF.	DEBIT	CREDIT	BALANCE	
					DEBIT	CREDIT

ACCOUNT   Food Supplies Expense   ACCOUNT NO. 524

DATE	ITEM	POST. REF.	DEBIT	CREDIT	BALANCE	
					DEBIT	CREDIT

Comprehensive Problem 1 (Continued)

ACCOUNT Phone Expense   ACCOUNT NO. 525

DATE	ITEM	POST. REF.	DEBIT	CREDIT	BALANCE DEBIT	BALANCE CREDIT

ACCOUNT Utilities Expense   ACCOUNT NO. 533

DATE	ITEM	POST. REF.	DEBIT	CREDIT	BALANCE DEBIT	BALANCE CREDIT

ACCOUNT Insurance Expense   ACCOUNT NO. 535

DATE	ITEM	POST. REF.	DEBIT	CREDIT	BALANCE DEBIT	BALANCE CREDIT

ACCOUNT Postage Expense   ACCOUNT NO. 536

DATE	ITEM	POST. REF.	DEBIT	CREDIT	BALANCE DEBIT	BALANCE CREDIT

ACCOUNT Depreciation Expense—Fishing Boats   ACCOUNT NO. 542

DATE	ITEM	POST. REF.	DEBIT	CREDIT	BALANCE DEBIT	BALANCE CREDIT

Comprehensive Problem 1 (Continued)
3. and 4.

	ACCOUNT TITLE	TRIAL BALANCE		ADJUSTMENTS	
		DEBIT	CREDIT	DEBIT	CREDIT
1					
2					
3					
4					
5					
6					
7					
8					
9					
10					
11					
12					
13					
14					
15					
16					
17					
18					
19					
20					
21					
22					
23					
24					
25					
26					
27					
28					
29					
30					
31					

Comprehensive Problem 1 (Continued)

ADJUSTED TRIAL BALANCE		INCOME STATEMENT		BALANCE SHEET		
DEBIT	CREDIT	DEBIT	CREDIT	DEBIT	CREDIT	
						1
						2
						3
						4
						5
						6
						7
						8
						9
						10
						11
						12
						13
						14
						15
						16
						17
						18
						19
						20
						21
						22
						23
						24
						25
						26
						27
						28
						29
						30
						31

Comprehensive Problem 1 (Continued)

7.

8.

Comprehensive Problem 1 (Continued)

9.

Comprehensive Problem 1 (Continued)
5. and 10.

GENERAL JOURNAL

PAGE 5

	DATE		DESCRIPTION	POST. REF.	DEBIT	CREDIT	
1							1
2							2
3							3
4							4
5							5
6							6
7							7
8							8
9							9
10							10
11							11
12							12
13							13
14							14
15							15
16							16
17							17
18							18
19							19
20							20
21							21
22							22
23							23
24							24
25							25
26							26
27							27
28							28
29							29
30							30
31							31
32							32
33							33
34							34
35							35

Comprehensive Problem 1 (Concluded)

GENERAL JOURNAL

	DATE		DESCRIPTION	POST. REF.	DEBIT	CREDIT	
1							1
2							2
3							3
4							4
5							5
6							6
7							7
8							8
9							9

12.

_____

_____

_____

ACCOUNT	ACCT. NO.	DEBIT BALANCE	CREDIT BALANCE

Comprehensive Problem 1, Period 2: The Accounting Cycle

1.

	DATE		DESCRIPTION	POST. REF.	DEBIT	CREDIT	
1							1
2							2
3							3
4							4
5							5
6							6
7							7
8							8
9							9
10							10
11							11
12							12
13							13
14							14
15							15
16							16
17							17
18							18
19							19
20							20
21							21
22							22
23							23
24							24
25							25
26							26
27							27
28							28
29							29
30							30
31							31
32							32
33							33
34							34
35							35

Comprehensive Problem 1, Period 2 (Continued)

GENERAL JOURNAL

	DATE	DESCRIPTION	POST. REF.	DEBIT	CREDIT	
1						1
2						2
3						3
4						4
5						5
6						6
7						7
8						8
9						9
10						10
11						11
12						12
13						13
14						14
15						15
16						16
17						17
18						18
19						19
20						20
21						21
22						22
23						23
24						24
25						25
26						26
27						27
28						28
29						29
30						30
31						31
32						32
33						33
34						34
35						35
36						36
37						37
38						38
39						39
40						40
41						41
42						42

Comprehensive Problem 1, Period 2 (Continued)

GENERAL JOURNAL

PAGE 7

	DATE	DESCRIPTION	POST. REF.	DEBIT	CREDIT	
1						1
2						2
3						3
4						4
5						5
6						6
7						7
8						8
9						9
10						10
11						11
12						12
13						13
14						14
15						15
16						16
17						17
18						18
19						19
20						20
21						21
22						22
23						23
24						24
25						25
26						26
27						27
28						28
29						29
30						30
31						31
32						32
33						33
34						34

Comprehensive Problem 1, Period 2 (Continued)

2., 6., and 11.

GENERAL LEDGER

ACCOUNT   Cash ACCOUNT NO.   101

DATE		ITEM	POST. REF.	DEBIT	CREDIT	BALANCE	
						DEBIT	CREDIT
20-- Apr.	30	Balance	✓			130 6 5 0 00	

ACCOUNT   Accounts Receivable ACCOUNT NO.   122

DATE	ITEM	POST. REF.	DEBIT	CREDIT	BALANCE	
					DEBIT	CREDIT

Comprehensive Problem 1, Period 2 (Continued)

ACCOUNT Office Supplies   ACCOUNT NO. 142

DATE		ITEM	POST. REF.	DEBIT	CREDIT	BALANCE DEBIT	BALANCE CREDIT
20-- Apr.	30	Balance	✔			1 0 0 00	

ACCOUNT Food Supplies   ACCOUNT NO. 144

DATE		ITEM	POST. REF.	DEBIT	CREDIT	BALANCE DEBIT	BALANCE CREDIT
20-- Apr.	30	Balance	✔			8 0 0 0 00	

ACCOUNT Prepaid Insurance   ACCOUNT NO. 145

DATE		ITEM	POST. REF.	DEBIT	CREDIT	BALANCE DEBIT	BALANCE CREDIT
20-- Apr.	30	Balance	✔			7 5 0 0 00	

ACCOUNT Prepaid Subscriptions   ACCOUNT NO. 146

DATE		ITEM	POST. REF.	DEBIT	CREDIT	BALANCE DEBIT	BALANCE CREDIT

Comprehensive Problem 1, Period 2 (Continued)

ACCOUNT Land   ACCOUNT NO. 161

DATE	ITEM	POST. REF.	DEBIT	CREDIT	BALANCE	
					DEBIT	CREDIT

ACCOUNT Buildings   ACCOUNT NO. 171

DATE	ITEM	POST. REF.	DEBIT	CREDIT	BALANCE	
					DEBIT	CREDIT

ACCOUNT Accumulated Depreciation—Buildings   ACCOUNT NO. 171.1

DATE	ITEM	POST. REF.	DEBIT	CREDIT	BALANCE	
					DEBIT	CREDIT

ACCOUNT Fishing Boats   ACCOUNT NO. 181

DATE		ITEM	POST. REF.	DEBIT	CREDIT	BALANCE	
						DEBIT	CREDIT
20-- Apr.	30	Balance	✔			60 0 0 0 00	

Comprehensive Problem 1, Period 2 (Continued)

ACCOUNT Accumulated Depreciation—Fishing Boats   ACCOUNT NO. 181.1

DATE		ITEM	POST. REF.	DEBIT	CREDIT	BALANCE DEBIT	BALANCE CREDIT
20-- Apr.	30	Balance	✓				1 0 0 0 00

ACCOUNT Surround Sound System   ACCOUNT NO. 182

DATE	ITEM	POST. REF.	DEBIT	CREDIT	BALANCE DEBIT	BALANCE CREDIT

ACCOUNT Accumulated Depreciation—Surround Sound System   ACCOUNT NO. 182.1

DATE	ITEM	POST. REF.	DEBIT	CREDIT	BALANCE DEBIT	BALANCE CREDIT

ACCOUNT Big Screen TV   ACCOUNT NO. 183

DATE	ITEM	POST. REF.	DEBIT	CREDIT	BALANCE DEBIT	BALANCE CREDIT

ACCOUNT Accumulated Depreciation—Big Screen TV   ACCOUNT NO. 183.1

DATE	ITEM	POST. REF.	DEBIT	CREDIT	BALANCE DEBIT	BALANCE CREDIT

Comprehensive Problem 1, Period 2 (Continued)

ACCOUNT Accounts Payable   ACCOUNT NO. 202

DATE		ITEM	POST. REF.	DEBIT	CREDIT	BALANCE DEBIT	BALANCE CREDIT
20-- Apr.	30	Balance	✔				66 5 0 0 00

ACCOUNT Wages Payable   ACCOUNT NO. 219

DATE		ITEM	POST. REF.	DEBIT	CREDIT	BALANCE DEBIT	BALANCE CREDIT
20-- Apr.	30	Balance	✔				5 0 0 00

ACCOUNT Bob Night, Capital   ACCOUNT NO. 311

DATE		ITEM	POST. REF.	DEBIT	CREDIT	BALANCE DEBIT	BALANCE CREDIT
20-- Apr.	30	Balance	✔				138 2 5 0 00

ACCOUNT Bob Night, Drawing   ACCOUNT NO. 312

DATE		ITEM	POST. REF.	DEBIT	CREDIT	BALANCE DEBIT	BALANCE CREDIT

Comprehensive Problem 1, Period 2 (Continued)

ACCOUNT   Income Summary   ACCOUNT NO.   313

DATE	ITEM	POST. REF.	DEBIT	CREDIT	BALANCE DEBIT	BALANCE CREDIT

ACCOUNT   Registration Fees   ACCOUNT NO.   401

DATE	ITEM	POST. REF.	DEBIT	CREDIT	BALANCE DEBIT	BALANCE CREDIT

ACCOUNT   Vending Commission Revenue   ACCOUNT NO.   404

DATE	ITEM	POST. REF.	DEBIT	CREDIT	BALANCE DEBIT	BALANCE CREDIT

ACCOUNT   Wages Expense   ACCOUNT NO.   511

DATE	ITEM	POST. REF.	DEBIT	CREDIT	BALANCE DEBIT	BALANCE CREDIT

Comprehensive Problem 1, Period 2 (Continued)

ACCOUNT Advertising Expense   ACCOUNT NO. 512

DATE	ITEM	POST. REF.	DEBIT	CREDIT	BALANCE	
					DEBIT	CREDIT

ACCOUNT Rent Expense   ACCOUNT NO. 521

DATE	ITEM	POST. REF.	DEBIT	CREDIT	BALANCE	
					DEBIT	CREDIT

ACCOUNT Office Supplies Expense   ACCOUNT NO. 523

DATE	ITEM	POST. REF.	DEBIT	CREDIT	BALANCE	
					DEBIT	CREDIT

ACCOUNT Food Supplies Expense   ACCOUNT NO. 524

DATE	ITEM	POST. REF.	DEBIT	CREDIT	BALANCE	
					DEBIT	CREDIT

Comprehensive Problem 1, Period 2 (Continued)

ACCOUNT Phone Expense   ACCOUNT NO. 525

DATE	ITEM	POST. REF.	DEBIT	CREDIT	BALANCE DEBIT	BALANCE CREDIT

ACCOUNT Utilities Expense   ACCOUNT NO. 533

DATE	ITEM	POST. REF.	DEBIT	CREDIT	BALANCE DEBIT	BALANCE CREDIT

ACCOUNT Insurance Expense   ACCOUNT NO. 535

DATE	ITEM	POST. REF.	DEBIT	CREDIT	BALANCE DEBIT	BALANCE CREDIT

ACCOUNT Postage Expense   ACCOUNT NO. 536

DATE	ITEM	POST. REF.	DEBIT	CREDIT	BALANCE DEBIT	BALANCE CREDIT

Comprehensive Problem 1, Period 2 (Continued)

ACCOUNT   Repair Expense   ACCOUNT NO.   537

DATE	ITEM	POST. REF.	DEBIT	CREDIT	BALANCE DEBIT	BALANCE CREDIT

ACCOUNT   Depreciation Expense—Buildings   ACCOUNT NO.   540

DATE	ITEM	POST. REF.	DEBIT	CREDIT	BALANCE DEBIT	BALANCE CREDIT

ACCOUNT   Depreciation Expense—Surround Sound System   ACCOUNT NO.   541

DATE	ITEM	POST. REF.	DEBIT	CREDIT	BALANCE DEBIT	BALANCE CREDIT

ACCOUNT   Depreciation Expense—Fishing Boats   ACCOUNT NO.   542

DATE	ITEM	POST. REF.	DEBIT	CREDIT	BALANCE DEBIT	BALANCE CREDIT

Comprehensive Problem 1, Period 2 (Continued)

ACCOUNT Depreciation Expense—Big Screen TV   ACCOUNT NO.   543

DATE	ITEM	POST. REF.	DEBIT	CREDIT	BALANCE DEBIT	BALANCE CREDIT

ACCOUNT Satellite Programming Expense   ACCOUNT NO.   546

DATE	ITEM	POST. REF.	DEBIT	CREDIT	BALANCE DEBIT	BALANCE CREDIT

ACCOUNT Subscriptions Expense   ACCOUNT NO.   548

DATE	ITEM	POST. REF.	DEBIT	CREDIT	BALANCE DEBIT	BALANCE CREDIT

Comprehensive Problem 1, Period 2 (Continued)
3. and 4.

	ACCOUNT TITLE	TRIAL BALANCE		ADJUSTMENTS	
		DEBIT	CREDIT	DEBIT	CREDIT
1					
2					
3					
4					
5					
6					
7					
8					
9					
10					
11					
12					
13					
14					
15					
16					
17					
18					
19					
20					
21					
22					
23					
24					
25					
26					
27					
28					
29					
30					
31					
32					
33					
34					
35					
36					
37					
38					
39					
40					

Comprehensive Problem 1, Period 2 (Continued)

ADJUSTED TRIAL BALANCE		INCOME STATEMENT		BALANCE SHEET		
DEBIT	CREDIT	DEBIT	CREDIT	DEBIT	CREDIT	
						1
						2
						3
						4
						5
						6
						7
						8
						9
						10
						11
						12
						13
						14
						15
						16
						17
						18
						19
						20
						21
						22
						23
						24
						25
						26
						27
						28
						29
						30
						31
						32
						33
						34
						35
						36
						37
						38
						39
						40

Comprehensive Problem 1, Period 2 (Continued)
5.

GENERAL JOURNAL   PAGE 8

	DATE	DESCRIPTION	POST. REF.	DEBIT	CREDIT	
1						1
2						2
3						3
4						4
5						5
6						6
7						7
8						8
9						9
10						10
11						11
12						12
13						13
14						14
15						15
16						16
17						17
18						18
19						19
20						20
21						21
22						22
23						23
24						24
25						25
26						26
27						27
28						28
29						29
30						30
31						31
32						32
33						33
34						34
35						35

Comprehensive Problem 1, Period 2 (Continued)

7.

8.

Comprehensive Problem 1, Period 2 (Continued)

9.

Comprehensive Problem 1, Period 2 (Continued)

10.

GENERAL JOURNAL

	DATE		DESCRIPTION	POST. REF.	DEBIT	CREDIT	
1							1
2							2
3							3
4							4
5							5
6							6
7							7
8							8
9							9
10							10
11							11
12							12
13							13
14							14
15							15
16							16
17							17
18							18
19							19
20							20
21							21
22							22
23							23
24							24
25							25
26							26
27							27
28							28
29							29
30							30
31							31
32							32
33							33
34							34
35							35

Comprehensive Problem 1, Period 2 (Concluded)

12.

ACCOUNT TITLE	ACCT. NO.	DEBIT BALANCE	CREDIT BALANCE

Exercise 7-1A

1. _____   5. _____

2. _____   6. _____

3. _____   7. _____

4. _____

Exercise 7-2A

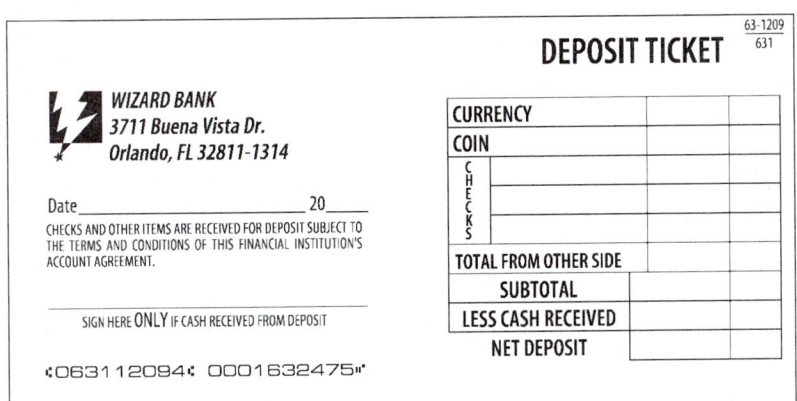

Exercise 7-3A

No. **1**			
DATE _____ 20 ____			
TO _____			
FOR _____			
ACCT. _____			

	DOLLARS	CENTS
BAL BRO'T FOR'D		
AMT. DEPOSITED		
TOTAL		
AMT. THIS CHECK		
BAL CAR'D FOR'D		

No. **1**   63-1209 / 631

_____ 20 _____

PAY
TO THE
ORDER OF _____ $ _____

_____ Dollars

WIZARD BANK
3711 Buena Vista Dr.
Orlando, FL 32811-1314

FOR CLASSROOM USE ONLY

MEMO _____   BY _____

⑆063112094⑆ 0001632475⑈

Exercise 7-4A

	Ending Bank Balance	Ending Check-book Balance
1.		
2.		
3.		
4.		
5.		
6.		
7.		

Exercise 7-5A

GENERAL JOURNAL

PAGE _____

	DATE		DESCRIPTION	POST. REF.	DEBIT	CREDIT	
1							1
2							2
3							3
4							4
5							5
6							6
7							7
8							8
9							9
10							10
11							11
12							12
13							13
14							14
15							15
16							16
17							17
18							18
19							19
20							20
21							21

Exercise 7-6A

GENERAL JOURNAL

PAGE

	DATE		DESCRIPTION	POST. REF.	DEBIT	CREDIT	
1							1
2							2
3							3
4							4
5							5
6							6
7							7
8							8
9							9
10							10
11							11
12							12
13							13
14							14
15							15
16							16
17							17
18							18
19							19
20							20
21							21
22							22
23							23
24							24
25							25
26							26
27							27
28							28
29							29
30							30
31							31
32							32
33							33
34							34
35							35
36							36

Exercise 7-7A

GENERAL JOURNAL   PAGE

	DATE	DESCRIPTION	POST. REF.	DEBIT	CREDIT	
1						1
2						2
3						3
4						4
5						5
6						6
7						7
8						8
9						9
10						10
11						11
12						12
13						13
14						14
15						15
16						16
17						17
18						18
19						19
20						20
21						21
22						22
23						23
24						24
25						25
26						26
27						27
28						28
29						29
30						30
31						31
32						32
33						33
34						34
35						35
36						36

Problem 7-8A

1.

Problem 7-8A (Concluded)
2.

GENERAL JOURNAL   PAGE

	DATE	DESCRIPTION	POST. REF.	DEBIT	CREDIT	
1						1
2						2
3						3
4						4
5						5
6						6
7						7
8						8
9						9
10						10
11						11
12						12
13						13
14						14
15						15

Problem 7-9A

1.

Problem 7-9A (Concluded)

2.

GENERAL JOURNAL   PAGE

	DATE		DESCRIPTION	POST. REF.	DEBIT	CREDIT	
1							1
2							2
3							3
4							4
5							5
6							6
7							7
8							8
9							9
10							10
11							11
12							12
13							13
14							14
15							15
16							16
17							17
18							18
19							19

Problem 7-10A

1. and 3.

GENERAL JOURNAL   PAGE

	DATE		DESCRIPTION	POST. REF.	DEBIT	CREDIT	
1							1
2							2
3							3
4							4
5							5
6							6
7							7
8							8
9							9
10							10
11							11
12							12
13							13

Problem 7-10A (Concluded)
2. and 3.

PETTY CASH PAYMENTS FOR MONTH OF _____ 20-- _____ PAGE _____

DAY	DESCRIPTION	VOU. NO.	TOTAL AMOUNT	OFFICE SUPPLIES	POSTAGE EXPENSE	CHARIT. CONTRIB. EXPENSE	PHONE EXPENSE	TRAVEL & ENTER. EXPENSE	MISC. EXPENSE	ACCOUNT	AMOUNT	
												1
												2
												3
												4
												5
												6
												7
												8
												9
												10
												11
												12
												13
												14
												15
												16
												17
												18
												19
												20
												21
												22

DISTRIBUTION OF PAYMENTS

Problem 7-11A

1.

GENERAL JOURNAL   PAGE 8

	DATE	DESCRIPTION	POST. REF.	DEBIT	CREDIT	
1						1
2						2
3						3
4						4
5						5
6						6
7						7
8						8
9						9
10						10
11						11
12						12
13						13
14						14
15						15
16						16
17						17
18						18
19						19
20						20
21						21
22						22
23						23

2.

ACCOUNT   ACCOUNT NO.

DATE	ITEM	POST. REF.	DEBIT	CREDIT	BALANCE DEBIT	BALANCE CREDIT

3. The balance represents:

Exercise 7-1B

1. _____   5. _____

2. _____   6. _____

3. _____   7. _____

4. _____

Exercise 7-2B

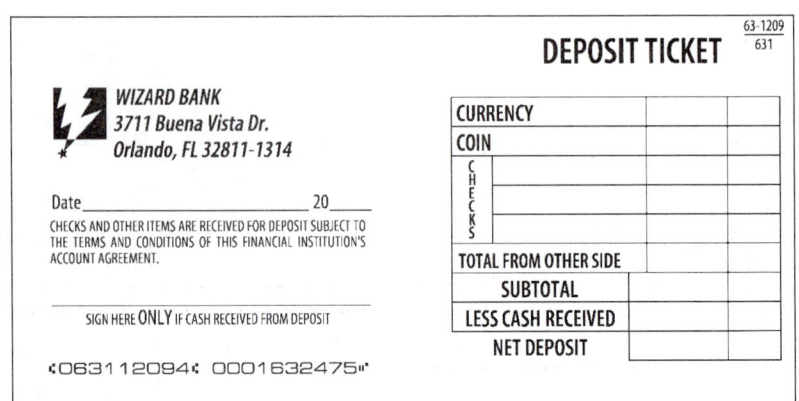

DEPOSIT TICKET $\frac{63\text{-}1209}{631}$

WIZARD BANK
3711 Buena Vista Dr.
Orlando, FL 32811-1314

Date_____ 20_____

CHECKS AND OTHER ITEMS ARE RECEIVED FOR DEPOSIT SUBJECT TO THE TERMS AND CONDITIONS OF THIS FINANCIAL INSTITUTION'S ACCOUNT AGREEMENT.

SIGN HERE ONLY IF CASH RECEIVED FROM DEPOSIT

⑈063112094⑈ 0001632475⑈

CURRENCY		
COIN		
C H E C K S		
TOTAL FROM OTHER SIDE		
SUBTOTAL		
LESS CASH RECEIVED		
NET DEPOSIT		

Exercise 7-3B

No. 1

DATE _____ 20_____

TO _____

FOR _____

ACCT. _____

	DOLLARS	CENTS
BAL BRO'T FOR'D		
AMT. DEPOSITED		
TOTAL		
AMT. THIS CHECK		
BAL CAR'D FOR'D		

No. 1 $\frac{63\text{-}1209}{631}$

_____ 20_____

PAY
TO THE
ORDER OF_____ $_____

_____ Dollars

WIZARD BANK   FOR CLASSROOM USE ONLY
3711 Buena Vista Dr.
Orlando, FL 32811-1314

MEMO_____   BY _____

⑈063112094⑈ 0001632475⑈

Exercise 7-4B

	Ending Bank **Balance**	Ending Check- **book Balance**
1.	_____	_____
2.	_____	_____
3.	_____	_____
4.	_____	_____
5.	_____	_____
6.	_____	_____
7.	_____	_____

Exercise 7-5B

GENERAL JOURNAL   PAGE _____

	DATE		DESCRIPTION	POST. REF.	DEBIT	CREDIT	
1							1
2							2
3							3
4							4
5							5
6							6
7							7
8							8
9							9
10							10
11							11
12							12
13							13
14							14
15							15
16							16
17							17
18							18
19							19
20							20
21							21

Exercise 7-6B

GENERAL JOURNAL

PAGE

	DATE		DESCRIPTION	POST. REF.	DEBIT	CREDIT	
1							1
2							2
3							3
4							4
5							5
6							6
7							7
8							8
9							9
10							10
11							11
12							12
13							13
14							14
15							15
16							16
17							17
18							18
19							19
20							20
21							21
22							22
23							23
24							24
25							25
26							26
27							27
28							28
29							29
30							30
31							31
32							32
33							33
34							34
35							35
36							36

Name _____

Exercise 7-7B

GENERAL JOURNAL

PAGE

	DATE		DESCRIPTION	POST. REF.	DEBIT	CREDIT	
1							1
2							2
3							3
4							4
5							5
6							6
7							7
8							8
9							9
10							10
11							11
12							12
13							13
14							14
15							15
16							16
17							17
18							18
19							19
20							20
21							21
22							22
23							23
24							24
25							25
26							26
27							27
28							28
29							29
30							30
31							31
32							32
33							33
34							34
35							35
36							36

Problem 7-8B

1.

Problem 7-8B (Concluded)
2.

GENERAL JOURNAL   PAGE _____

	DATE		DESCRIPTION	POST. REF.	DEBIT	CREDIT	
1							1
2							2
3							3
4							4
5							5
6							6
7							7
8							8
9							9
10							10
11							11
12							12
13							13
14							14
15							15

Problem 7-9B

1.

Problem 7-9B (Concluded)

2.

GENERAL JOURNAL

PAGE _____

	DATE		DESCRIPTION	POST. REF.	DEBIT	CREDIT	
1							1
2							2
3							3
4							4
5							5
6							6
7							7
8							8
9							9
10							10
11							11
12							12
13							13
14							14
15							15
16							16
17							17
18							18
19							19

Problem 7-10B

1. and 3.

GENERAL JOURNAL PAGE

	DATE		DESCRIPTION	POST. REF.	DEBIT	CREDIT	
1							1
2							2
3							3
4							4
5							5
6							6
7							7
8							8
9							9
10							10
11							11
12							12
13							13

Problem 7-10B (Concluded)

2. and 3.

PETTY CASH PAYMENTS FOR MONTH OF _____ 20-- PAGE _____

| DAY | DESCRIPTION | VOU. NO. | TOTAL AMOUNT | DISTRIBUTION OF PAYMENTS | | | | | | ACCOUNT | AMOUNT |
				OFFICE SUPPLIES	POSTAGE EXPENSE	CHARIT. CONTRIB. EXPENSE	PHONE EXPENSE	TRAVEL & ENTER. EXPENSE	MISC. EXPENSE		
1											
2											
3											
4											
5											
6											
7											
8											
9											
10											
11											
12											
13											
14											
15											
16											
17											
18											
19											
20											
21											
22											

Problem 7-11B

1.

GENERAL JOURNAL

PAGE   8

	DATE	DESCRIPTION	POST. REF.	DEBIT	CREDIT	
1						1
2						2
3						3
4						4
5						5
6						6
7						7
8						8
9						9
10						10
11						11
12						12
13						13
14						14
15						15
16						16
17						17
18						18
19						19
20						20
21						21
22						22
23						23

2.

ACCOUNT

ACCOUNT NO.

DATE	ITEM	POST. REF.	DEBIT	CREDIT	BALANCE	
					DEBIT	CREDIT

3. The balance represents:

Mastery Problem

1.

PETTY CASH PAYMENTS FOR MONTH OF _____ 20--   PAGE _____

DAY	DESCRIPTION	VOU. NO.	TOTAL AMOUNT	TRUCK EXPENSE	POSTAGE EXPENSE	CHARIT. CONTRIB. EXPENSE	PHONE EXPENSE	ADVERT. EXPENSE	MISC. EXPENSE	ACCOUNT	AMOUNT	

DISTRIBUTION OF PAYMENTS

Rows numbered 1 through 22.

Mastery Problem (Continued)
2. and 3.

GENERAL JOURNAL

	DATE		DESCRIPTION	POST. REF.	DEBIT	CREDIT	
1							1
2							2
3							3
4							4
5							5
6							6
7							7
8							8
9							9
10							10
11							11
12							12
13							13
14							14
15							15
16							16
17							17
18							18
19							19
20							20
21							21
22							22
23							23
24							24
25							25
26							26
27							27
28							28
29							29
30							30
31							31
32							32
33							33
34							34
35							35

Mastery Problem (Concluded)

GENERAL JOURNAL

	DATE	DESCRIPTION	POST. REF.	DEBIT	CREDIT	
1						1
2						2
3						3
4						4
5						5
6						6
7						7
8						8
9						9
10						10
11						11
12						12
13						13
14						14

3.

		DEBIT	CREDIT

Challenge Problem
1. Panera Bakery

GENERAL JOURNAL   PAGE

	DATE		DESCRIPTION	POST. REF.	DEBIT	CREDIT	
1							1
2							2
3							3
4							4
5							5
6							6
7							7
8							8
9							9
10							10
11							11
12							12
13							13
14							14
15							15
16							16
17							17
18							18
19							19
20							20
21							21
22							22
23							23
24							24
25							25
26							26
27							27
28							28
29							29

Challenge Problem (Concluded)

2. Lawrence Bank

GENERAL JOURNAL   PAGE _____

	DATE	DESCRIPTION	POST. REF.	DEBIT	CREDIT	
1						1
2						2
3						3
4						4
5						5
6						6
7						7
8						8
9						9
10						10
11						11
12						12
13						13
14						14
15						15
16						16
17						17
18						18
19						19
20						20
21						21
22						22
23						23
24						24
25						25
26						26
27						27
28						28
29						29

APPENDIX: Internal Controls

Exercise 7Apx-1A

1. _____

   _____

2. _____

   _____

3. _____

   _____

4. _____

   _____

5. _____

   _____

Exercise 7Apx-2A

1. _____

2. _____

3. _____

4. _____

5. _____

Exercise 7Apx-3A

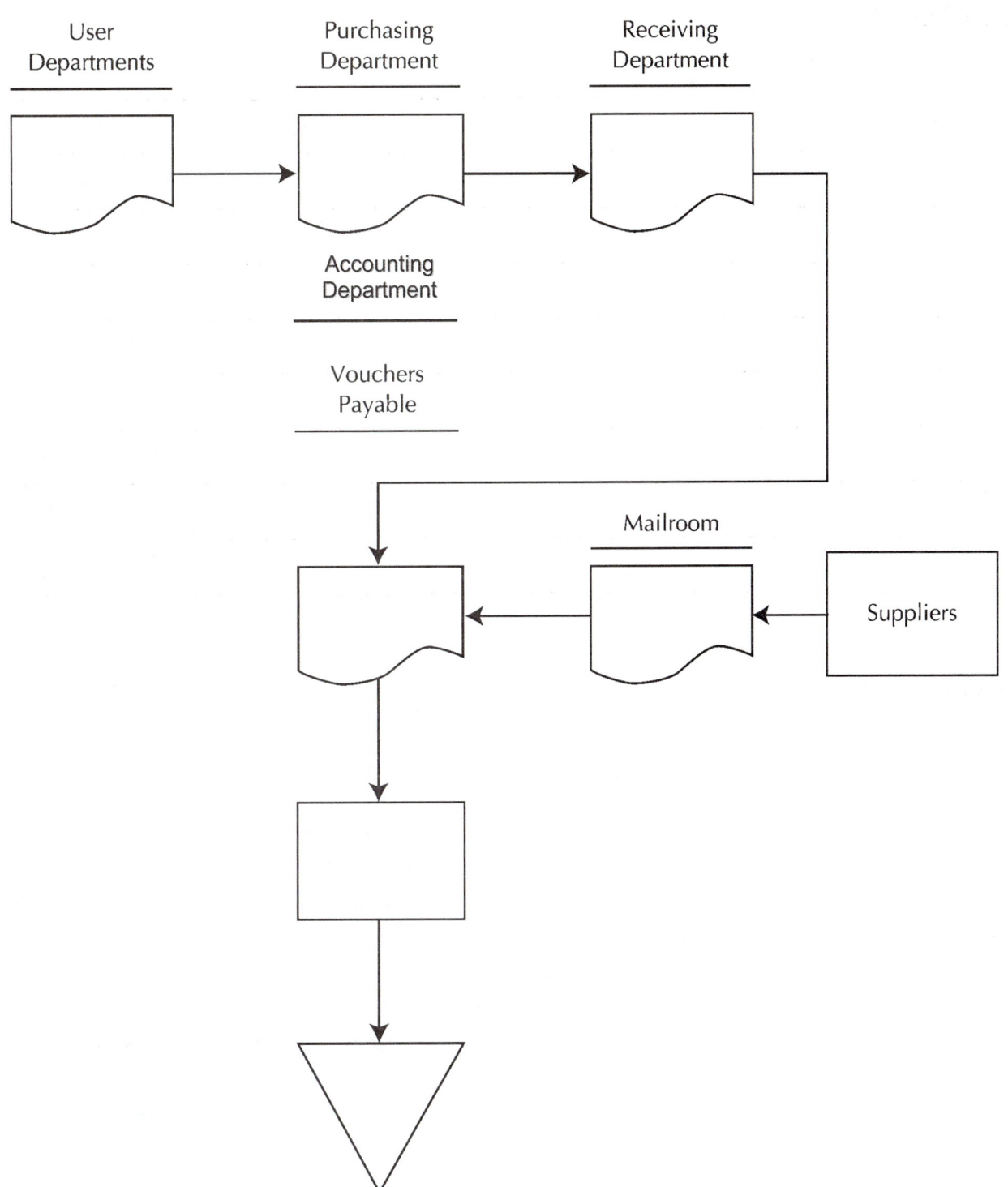

User
Departments

Purchasing
Department

Receiving
Department

Accounting
Department

Vouchers
Payable

Mailroom

Suppliers

Problem 7Apx-4A

1. _____

_____

2. _____

_____

3. _____

_____

4. _____

_____

Exercise 7Apx-1B

1. _____

_____

2. _____

_____

3. _____

_____

4. _____

_____

Exercise 7Apx-2B

1. _____

2. _____

3. _____

4. _____

Exercise 7Apx-3B

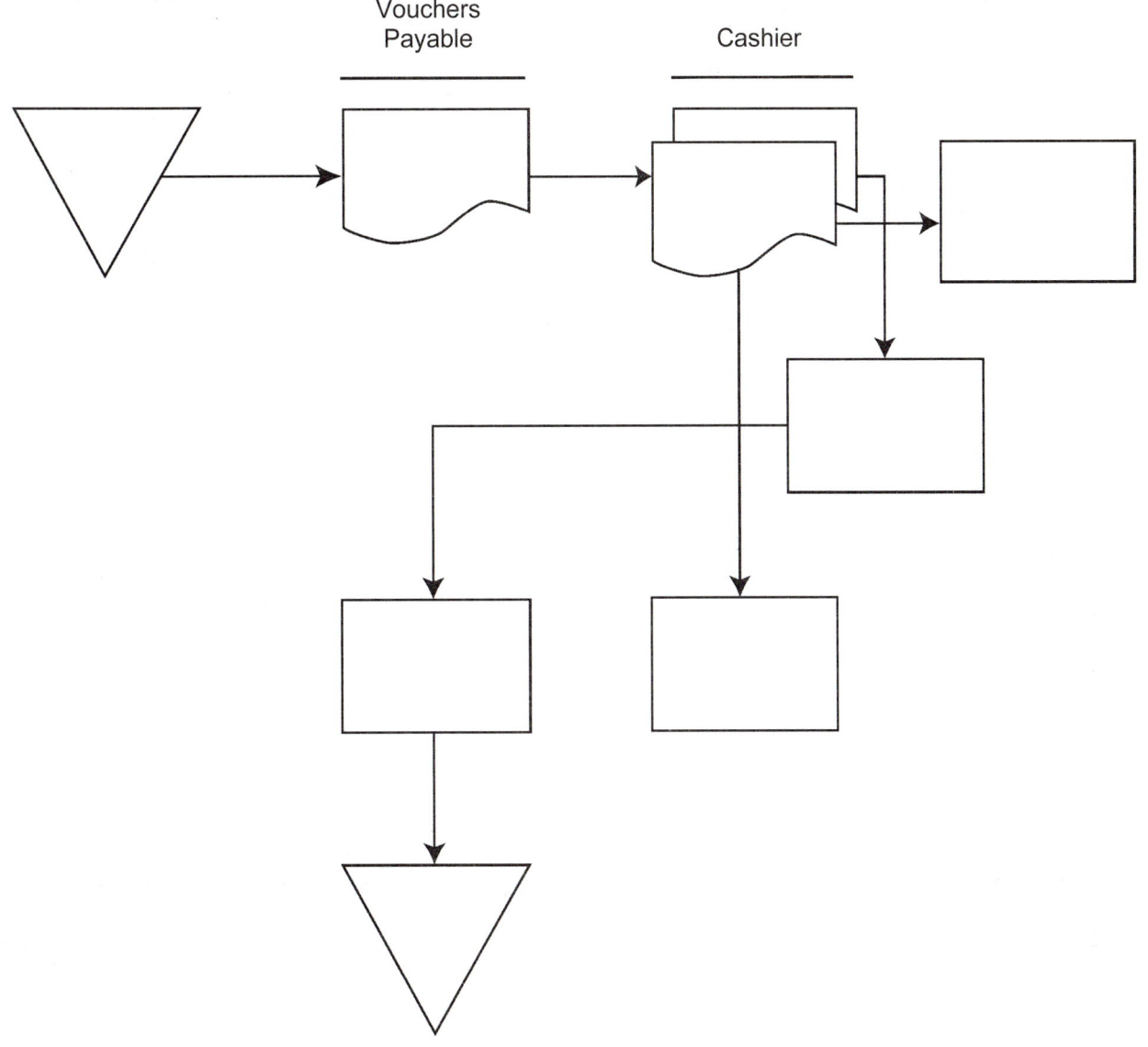

Problem 7Apx-4B

1. _____

_____

2. _____

_____

3. _____

_____

4. _____

_____

Exercise 8-1A

_____

_____

_____

_____

Exercise 8-2A

_____

_____

_____

_____

_____

_____

_____

Exercise 8-3A

	Marital Status	Total Weekly Earnings	Number of Allowances	Amount of Withholding
a.	S	$347.60	2	_____
b.	S	451.50	1	_____
c.	M	481.15	3	_____
d.	S	490.52	0	_____
e.	M	691.89	5	_____

Exercise 8-4A

Cumul. Pay Before Current Weekly Payroll	Current Gross Pay	Year-to-Date Earnings	Soc. Sec. Maximum	Amount Over Max. Soc. Sec.	Amount Subject to Soc. Sec.	Soc. Sec. Tax Withheld	Medicare Tax Withheld
$ 22,000	$1,700	_____	$118,500	_____	_____	_____	_____
54,000	4,200	_____	118,500	_____	_____	_____	_____
115,900	3,925	_____	118,500	_____	_____	_____	_____
117,900	4,600	_____	118,500	_____	_____	_____	_____

Exercise 8-5A

a. _____ regular hours × $10 per hour _____

b. _____ overtime hours × $15 per hour _____

c. Total gross wages _____

d. Federal income tax withholding (from tax tables in Figure 8-4) _____

e. Social Security withholding at 6.2% _____

f. Medicare withholding at 1.45% _____

g. Total withholding _____

h. Net pay _____

Exercise 8-6A

GENERAL JOURNAL PAGE _____

	DATE	DESCRIPTION	POST. REF.	DEBIT	CREDIT	
1						1
2						2
3						3
4						4
5						5
6						6
7						7
8						8
9						9

Exercise 8-7A

GENERAL JOURNAL PAGE _____

	DATE	DESCRIPTION	POST. REF.	DEBIT	CREDIT	
1						1
2						2
3						3
4						4
5						5
6						6
7						7
8						8
9						9

Problem 8-8A

1.

_____

_____

_____

_____

_____

_____

_____

_____

_____

_____

_____

_____

_____

_____

_____

_____

_____

_____

_____

2.

GENERAL JOURNAL

PAGE

	DATE	DESCRIPTION	POST. REF.	DEBIT	CREDIT	
1						1
2						2
3						3
4						4
5						5
6						6
7						7
8						8
9						9
10						10
11						11
12						12
13						13
14						14
15						15

Problem 8-9A

1.

PAYROLL REGISTER

	NAME	NO. ALLOW.	MARIT. STATUS	EARNINGS					CUMULATIVE TOTAL	TAXABLE EARNINGS		
				REGULAR		OVERTIME		TOTAL		UNEMPLOY. COMP.		SOCIAL SECURITY
1												
2												
3												
4												
5												
6												
7												
8												
9												
10												
11												
12												
13												
14												

Problem 8-9A (Concluded)

FOR PERIOD ENDED 20--

				DEDUCTIONS				
FEDERAL INCOME TAX	SOCIAL SECURITY TAX	MEDICARE TAX	CITY TAX	HEALTH INSUR.	OTHER	TOTAL	NET PAY	CK. NO.
								1
								2
								3
								4
								5
								6
								7
								8
								9
								10
								11
								12
								13
								14

2.

GENERAL JOURNAL

PAGE

	DATE	DESCRIPTION	POST. REF.	DEBIT	CREDIT	
1						1
2						2
3						3
4						4
5						5
6						6
7						7
8						8
9						9
10						10
11						11
12						12
13						13
14						14

Problem 8-10A

EMPLOYEE EARNINGS RECORD

20 -- PERIOD ENDED	EARNINGS						TAXABLE EARNINGS			DEDUCTIONS			
	REGULAR		OVERTIME		TOTAL	CUMULATIVE TOTAL	UNEMPLOY. COMP.		SOCIAL SECURITY	FEDERAL INCOME TAX		SOCIAL SECURITY TAX	
GENDER	DEPARTMENT			OCCUPATION			SOCIAL SECURITY NO.			MARITAL STATUS		ALLOW- ANCES	
M	F												

Problem 8-10A (Concluded)

FOR PERIOD ENDED   20--

MEDICARE TAX	CITY TAX	HEALTH INSURANCE	DEDUCTIONS					TOTAL	CK. NO.	AMOUNT	
			OTHER								
PAY RATE	DATE OF BIRTH	DATE HIRED	NAME/ADDRESS							EMP. NO.	

Exercise 8-1B

_____
_____
_____
_____

Exercise 8-2B

_____
_____
_____
_____
_____
_____
_____
_____

Exercise 8-3B

	Marital Status	Total Weekly Earnings	Number of Allowances	Amount of Withholding
a.	M	$546.00	4	_____
b.	M	390.00	1	_____
c.	S	461.39	2	_____
d.	M	522.88	2	_____
e.	S	612.00	0	_____

Exercise 8-4B

Cumul. Pay Before Current Weekly Payroll	Current Gross Pay	Year-to-Date Earnings	Soc. Sec. Maximum	Amount Over Max. Soc. Sec.	Amount Subject to Soc. Sec.	Soc. Sec. Tax Withheld	Medicare Tax Withheld
$ 31,000	$1,500	_____	$118,500	_____	_____	_____	_____
53,000	2,860	_____	118,500	_____	_____	_____	_____
115,600	3,140	_____	118,500	_____	_____	_____	_____
117,900	2,920	_____	118,500	_____	_____	_____	_____

Exercise 8-5B

a. _____ regular hours × $12 per hour

b. _____ overtime hours × $18 per hour   _____

c. Total gross wages   _____

d. Federal income tax withholding (from tax tables in Figure 8-4) _____

e. Social Security withholding at 6.2%   _____

f. Medicare withholding at 1.45%   _____

g. Total withholding   _____

h. Net pay   _____

Exercise 8-6B

GENERAL JOURNAL   PAGE

	DATE	DESCRIPTION	POST. REF.	DEBIT	CREDIT	
1						1
2						2
3						3
4						4
5						5
6						6
7						7
8						8
9						9
10						10
11						11
12						12
13						13
14						14
15						15
16						16
17						17
18						18
19						19
20						20
21						21
22						22

Exercise 8-7B

GENERAL JOURNAL

	DATE	DESCRIPTION	POST. REF.	DEBIT	CREDIT	
1						1
2						2
3						3
4						4
5						5
6						6
7						7
8						8
9						9
10						10
11						11
12						12
13						13

Problem 8-8B

1.

Problem 8-8B (Concluded)

2.

GENERAL JOURNAL

	DATE		DESCRIPTION	POST. REF.	DEBIT	CREDIT	
1							1
2							2
3							3
4							4
5							5
6							6
7							7
8							8
9							9
10							10
11							11
12							12
13							13
14							14
15							15
16							16
17							17
18							18
19							19
20							20
21							21
22							22
23							23
24							24
25							25
26							26
27							27
28							28
29							29
30							30
31							31
32							32
33							33
34							34
35							35

Problem 8-9B

1.

PAYROLL REGISTER

	NAME	NO. ALLOW.	MARIT. STATUS	EARNINGS						CUMULATIVE TOTAL		TAXABLE EARNINGS			
				REGULAR		OVERTIME		TOTAL				UNEMPLOY. COMP.		SOCIAL SECURITY	
1															
2															
3															
4															
5															
6															
7															
8															
9															
10															
11															
12															
13															
14															

Problem 8-9B (Concluded)

FOR PERIOD ENDED   20--

	FEDERAL INCOME TAX		SOCIAL SECURITY TAX		MEDICARE TAX		CITY TAX		HEALTH INSUR.		OTHER			TOTAL		NET PAY		CK. NO.	
																			1
																			2
																			3
																			4
																			5
																			6
																			7
																			8
																			9
																			10
																			11
																			12
																			13
																			14

2.

GENERAL JOURNAL

    PAGE

	DATE		DESCRIPTION	POST. REF.	DEBIT	CREDIT	
1							1
2							2
3							3
4							4
5							5
6							6
7							7
8							8
9							9
10							10
11							11
12							12
13							13
14							14

Problem 8-10B

EMPLOYEE EARNINGS RECORD

| 20 -- PERIOD ENDED | EARNINGS | | | | | | TAXABLE EARNINGS | | | | DEDUCTIONS | | | | |
	REGULAR		OVERTIME		TOTAL	CUMULATIVE TOTAL	UNEMPLOY. COMP.		SOCIAL SECURITY		FEDERAL INCOME TAX		SOCIAL SECURITY TAX		

GENDER		DEPARTMENT	OCCUPATION	SOCIAL SECURITY NO.	MARITAL STATUS	ALLOW-ANCES
M	F					

Problem 8-10B (Concluded)

FOR PERIOD ENDED 20--

MEDICARE TAX		CITY TAX		HEALTH INSURANCE		DEDUCTIONS OTHER			TOTAL		CK. NO.	AMOUNT	

PAY RATE	DATE OF BIRTH	DATE HIRED	NAME/ADDRESS	EMP. NO.

Mastery Problem

1.

PAYROLL REGISTER

	NAME	NO. ALLOW.	MARIT. STATUS	EARNINGS				TAXABLE EARNINGS	
				REGULAR	OVERTIME	TOTAL	CUMULATIVE TOTAL	UNEMPLOY. COMP.	SOCIAL SECURITY
1									
2									
3									
4									
5									
6									
7									
8									
9									
10									
11									
12									
13									
14									

3.

EMPLOYEE EARNINGS RECORD

20 -- PERIOD ENDED	EARNINGS				TAXABLE EARNINGS		FEDERAL INCOME TAX
	REGULAR	OVERTIME	TOTAL	CUMULATIVE TOTAL	UNEMPLOY. COMP.	SOCIAL SECURITY	
11/4	330 00	33 00	363 00	6,145 50	363 00	363 00	5 00
11/11	440 00	49 50	489 50	6,635 00	489 50	489 50	17 00
11/18							
11/25							

GENDER		DEPARTMENT	OCCUPATION	SOCIAL SECURITY NO.	MARITAL STATUS
M	F				

Mastery Problem (Continued)

FOR PERIOD ENDED 20--

				DEDUCTIONS									
FEDERAL INCOME TAX		SOCIAL SECURITY TAX		MEDICARE TAX		STATE INCOME TAX		HEALTH INSURANCE		CREDIT UNION		TOTAL		NET PAY		CK. NO.	
																	1
																	2
																	3
																	4
																	5
																	6
																	7
																	8
																	9
																	10
																	11
																	12
																	13
																	14

FOR PERIOD ENDED 20--

	DEDUCTIONS								NET PAY		
SOCIAL SECURITY TAX		MEDICARE TAX		STATE INCOME TAX		HEALTH INSURANCE		CREDIT UNION		TOTAL		CK. NO.		AMOUNT	
22	51	5	26	12	71			72	60	118	08	121	244	92
30	35	7	10	17	13			97	90	169	48	229	320	02

ALLOWANCES	PAY RATE	DATE OF BIRTH	DATE HIRED	NAME/ADDRESS	EMP. NO.

Mastery Problem (Concluded)

2.

GENERAL JOURNAL

PAGE

	DATE	DESCRIPTION	POST. REF.	DEBIT	CREDIT	
1						1
2						2
3						3
4						4
5						5
6						6
7						7
8						8
9						9
10						10
11						11
12						12
13						13
14						14
15						15
16						16
17						17
18						18
19						19
20						20
21						21
22						22
23						23
24						24
25						25
26						26
27						27
28						28
29						29
30						30
31						31
32						32
33						33
34						34
35						35

Challenge Problem

1.

GENERAL JOURNAL

PAGE

	DATE	DESCRIPTION	POST. REF.	DEBIT	CREDIT	
1						1
2						2
3						3
4						4
5						5
6						6
7						7
8						8
9						9
10						10

2.

Exercise 9-1A

_____
_____
_____
_____
_____

GENERAL JOURNAL   PAGE

	DATE		DESCRIPTION	POST. REF.	DEBIT	CREDIT	
1							1
2							2
3							3
4							4
5							5
6							6
7							7

Exercise 9-2A

_____
_____
_____
_____
_____
_____
_____
_____

GENERAL JOURNAL   PAGE

	DATE		DESCRIPTION	POST. REF.	DEBIT	CREDIT	
1							1
2							2
3							3
4							4
5							5
6							6
7							7

Exercise 9-3A

Name	Current Earnings	Taxable Earnings Unemploy. Comp.	Social Security
Jordahl			
Keesling			
Palmer			
Soltis			
Stout			
Xia			
Total			

GENERAL JOURNAL   PAGE

	DATE		DESCRIPTION	POST. REF.	DEBIT	CREDIT	
1							1
2							2
3							3
4							4
5							5
6							6
7							7

Exercise 9-4A

Exercise 9-5A

GENERAL JOURNAL   PAGE _____

	DATE	DESCRIPTION	POST. REF.	DEBIT	CREDIT	
1						1
2						2
3						3
4						4
5						5
6						6
7						7
8						8
9						9
10						10
11						11
12						12

Exercise 9-6A

1.

GENERAL JOURNAL   PAGE _____

	DATE	DESCRIPTION	POST. REF.	DEBIT	CREDIT	
1						1
2						2
3						3
4						4
5						5

2.

_____

_____

_____

_____

GENERAL JOURNAL   PAGE _____

	DATE	DESCRIPTION	POST. REF.	DEBIT	CREDIT	
1						1
2						2
3						3
4						4

Problem 9-7A

1.

		Taxable Earnings	
Name	**Current Earnings**	**Unemploy. Comp.**	**Social Security**
Click, Katelyn			
Coombs, Michelle			
Faus, Erin			
Lenihan, Marcus			
McMahon, Drew			
Newell, Marg			
Stevens, Matt			
Total			

2.

GENERAL JOURNAL

PAGE

	DATE	DESCRIPTION	POST. REF.	DEBIT	CREDIT	
1						1
2						2
3						3
4						4
5						5
6						6
7						7
8						8
9						9
10						10

Problem 9-8A
1.

GENERAL JOURNAL   PAGE _____

	DATE		DESCRIPTION	POST. REF.	DEBIT	CREDIT	
1							1
2							2
3							3
4							4
5							5
6							6
7							7
8							8
9							9
10							10
11							11
12							12
13							13
14							14
15							15
16							16
17							17
18							18
19							19
20							20
21							21
22							22
23							23
24							24
25							25
26							26
27							27
28							28
29							29
30							30
31							31
32							32
33							33
34							34
35							35
36							36

Problem 9-8A (Continued)

GENERAL JOURNAL

PAGE

	DATE	DESCRIPTION	POST. REF.	DEBIT	CREDIT	
1						1
2						2
3						3
4						4
5						5
6						6
7						7
8						8
9						9
10						10
11						11
12						12
13						13
14						14
15						15
16						16
17						17
18						18
19						19
20						20
21						21
22						22
23						23
24						24
25						25
26						26
27						27
28						28
29						29
30						30
31						31
32						32
33						33
34						34
35						35

Problem 9-8A (Concluded)

2.

Cash	101		Employee Federal Income Tax Payable 211

Social Security Tax Payable	212		Medicare Tax Payable	213

Savings Bond Deductions Payable	218		FUTA Tax Payable	221

SUTA Tax Payable	222		Wages and Salaries Expense	511

Payroll Taxes Expense	530

Problem 9-9A

1.

_____

_____

_____

_____

_____

_____

GENERAL JOURNAL

PAGE

	DATE		DESCRIPTION	POST. REF.	DEBIT	CREDIT	
1							1
2							2
3							3
4							4
5							5
6							6

2.

_____

_____

_____

_____

_____

_____

GENERAL JOURNAL

PAGE

	DATE		DESCRIPTION	POST. REF.	DEBIT	CREDIT	
1							1
2							2
3							3
4							4
5							5
6							6

Problem 9-9A (Concluded)

3.

_____

_____

_____

_____

_____

_____

GENERAL JOURNAL   PAGE _____

	DATE	DESCRIPTION	POST. REF.	DEBIT	CREDIT	
1						1
2						2
3						3
4						4
5						5

Exercise 9-1B

_____

_____

_____

_____

_____

_____

_____

GENERAL JOURNAL   PAGE _____

	DATE	DESCRIPTION	POST. REF.	DEBIT	CREDIT	
1						1
2						2
3						3
4						4
5						5
6						6
7						7
8						8
9						9

Exercise 9-2B

_____
_____
_____
_____
_____
_____
_____
_____
_____
_____
_____
_____

GENERAL JOURNAL   PAGE

	DATE	DESCRIPTION	POST. REF.	DEBIT	CREDIT	
1						1
2						2
3						3
4						4
5						5
6						6
7						7
8						8

Exercise 9-3B

		Taxable Earnings	
Name	**Current Earnings**	**Unemploy. Comp.**	**Social Security**
Carlson	_____	_____	_____
Delgado	_____	_____	_____
Lewis	_____	_____	_____
Nixon	_____	_____	_____
Shippe	_____	_____	_____
Watts	_____	_____	_____
Total	_____	_____	_____

Exercise 9-3B (Concluded)

_____

_____

_____

_____

_____

GENERAL JOURNAL   PAGE

	DATE	DESCRIPTION	POST. REF.	DEBIT	CREDIT	
1						1
2						2
3						3
4						4
5						5
6						6
7						7

Exercise 9-4B: See page WP-302.

Exercise 9-5B

GENERAL JOURNAL   PAGE

	DATE	DESCRIPTION	POST. REF.	DEBIT	CREDIT	
1						1
2						2
3						3
4						4
5						5
6						6
7						7
8						8
9						9
10						10
11						11
12						12
13						13
14						14

Exercise 9-4B

_____

_____

_____

_____

_____

_____

_____

_____

Exercise 9-6B

1.

GENERAL JOURNAL

PAGE

	DATE		DESCRIPTION	POST. REF.	DEBIT	CREDIT	
1							1
2							2
3							3
4							4
5							5

2.

_____

_____

_____

_____

_____

_____

GENERAL JOURNAL

PAGE

	DATE		DESCRIPTION	POST. REF.	DEBIT	CREDIT	
1							1
2							2
3							3
4							4
5							5

Problem 9-7B

1.

		Taxable Earnings	
Name	**Current Earnings**	**Unemploy. Comp.**	**Social Security**
Ackers, Alice	_____	_____	_____
Conley, Dorothy	_____	_____	_____
Davis, James	_____	_____	_____
Lawrence, Kevin	_____	_____	_____
Rawlings, Judy	_____	_____	_____
Tanaka, Sumio	_____	_____	_____
Vadillo, Raynette	_____	_____	_____
Total	_____	_____	_____

_____
_____
_____
_____
_____
_____
_____
_____

2.

GENERAL JOURNAL   PAGE _____

	DATE		DESCRIPTION	POST. REF.	DEBIT	CREDIT	
1							1
2							2
3							3
4							4
5							5
6							6
7							7
8							8
9							9
10							10
11							11
12							12

Problem 9-8B

1.

GENERAL JOURNAL

PAGE

	DATE		DESCRIPTION	POST. REF.	DEBIT	CREDIT	
1							1
2							2
3							3
4							4
5							5
6							6
7							7
8							8
9							9
10							10
11							11
12							12
13							13
14							14
15							15
16							16
17							17
18							18
19							19
20							20
21							21
22							22
23							23
24							24
25							25
26							26
27							27
28							28
29							29
30							30
31							31
32							32
33							33
34							34
35							35
36							36

Problem 9-8B (Continued)

GENERAL JOURNAL   PAGE _____

	DATE		DESCRIPTION	POST. REF.	DEBIT	CREDIT	
1							1
2							2
3							3
4							4
5							5
6							6
7							7
8							8
9							9
10							10
11							11
12							12
13							13
14							14
15							15
16							16
17							17
18							18
19							19
20							20
21							21
22							22
23							23
24							24
25							25
26							26
27							27
28							28
29							29
30							30
31							31
32							32
33							33
34							34
35							35

Problem 9-8B (Concluded)

2.

Cash	101		Employee Federal Income Tax Payable 211

Social Security Tax Payable	212		Medicare Tax Payable	213

Savings Bond Deductions Payable	218		FUTA Tax Payable	221

SUTA Tax Payable	222		Wages and Salaries Expense	511

Payroll Taxes Expense	530

Problem 9-9B

1.

_____
_____
_____
_____
_____
_____

GENERAL JOURNAL   PAGE _____

	DATE	DESCRIPTION	POST. REF.	DEBIT	CREDIT	
1						1
2						2
3						3
4						4
5						5
6						6

2.

_____
_____
_____
_____
_____
_____

GENERAL JOURNAL   PAGE _____

	DATE	DESCRIPTION	POST. REF.	DEBIT	CREDIT	
1						1
2						2
3						3
4						4
5						5
6						6

Problem 9-9B (Concluded)

3.

GENERAL JOURNAL   PAGE

	DATE		DESCRIPTION	POST. REF.	DEBIT	CREDIT	
1							1
2							2
3							3
4							4

Mastery Problem

1., 2., and 3.

GENERAL JOURNAL   PAGE

	DATE		DESCRIPTION	POST. REF.	DEBIT	CREDIT	
1							1
2							2
3							3
4							4
5							5
6							6
7							7
8							8
9							9
10							10
11							11
12							12
13							13
14							14
15							15
16							16
17							17
18							18
19							19
20							20
21							21
22							22
23							23
24							24
25							25
26							26
27							27
28							28
29							29
30							30
31							31
32							32
33							33
34							34
35							35

Mastery Problem (Concluded)

GENERAL JOURNAL

PAGE

	DATE	DESCRIPTION	POST. REF.	DEBIT	CREDIT	
1						1
2						2
3						3
4						4
5						5
6						6
7						7
8						8
9						9
10						10
11						11
12						12
13						13
14						14
15						15
16						16
17						17
18						18
19						19
20						20
21						21
22						22
23						23
24						24
25						25
26						26
27						27
28						28
29						29
30						30
31						31
32						32
33						33
34						34
35						35

Challenge Problem

1.

_____

_____

_____

_____

_____

2.

GENERAL JOURNAL   PAGE

	DATE		DESCRIPTION	POST. REF.	DEBIT	CREDIT	
1							1
2							2
3							3
4							4
5							5
6							6
7							7

3.

_____

_____

_____

_____

NOTES

NOTES

NOTES

END PAGE OF
WORKING PAPERS